SUE HACKMAN

# Hodder Reading Project

Acknowledgements for copyright text, photographs and images can be found on page 92.

*Hodder Headline's policy is to use papers that are natural, renewable and recyclable products and made from wood grown in sustainable forests. The logging and manufacturing processes are expected to conform to the environmental regulations of the country of origin.*

Orders: please contact Bookpoint Ltd, 130 Milton Park, Abingdon, Oxon OX14 4SB. Telephone: (44) 01235 827720. Fax: (44) 01235 400454. Lines are open from 9.00am to 5.00pm, Monday to Saturday, with a 24-hour message answering service. Visit our website at www.hoddereducation.co.uk


First published in 2006 by
Hodder Murray, an imprint of Hodder Education,
a member of the Hodder Headline Group
338 Euston Road
London NW1 3BH

Impression number 10 9 8 7 6 5 4 3 2
Year 2011 2010 2009 2008 2007



Cover photo: Rollerblader © A. T. Willett/Alamy.
Typeset by DC Graphic Design Ltd, Swanley Village, Kent.
Internal artwork © Barking Dog.
Printed in Italy.

A catalogue record for this title is available from the British Library

ISBN-10: 0 340 90478 X
ISBN-13: 9 780340 904787

# CONTENTS

# SECTION A
# Reading Strategies

## A1 Tracking your thoughts

In this masterclass you will learn how to:

- respond as you read
- capture your responses in a journal
- keep track of information as you read

### Responding to reading

When you read, your brain is busy. It tries to 'see' what is happening; it interrupts and asks questions; it passes comments. But that's not all…

As you read this paragraph, notice what your eyes and brain are doing.

They came suddenly, roaring round the village in four-wheel-drive trucks, horns blaring, shooting pointlessly into the morning sky. As soon as we heard the noise, we ran inside, closed the shutters and locked the doors. Mother and I hid in the cupboard under the stairs with my little brother and sisters. Father waited in the living room, alone.

It was so dark in the cupboard we couldn't even see each other's faces. We sat on the floor, holding the children's hands and telling them there was nothing to worry about because no one could find us in such a secret place. They were not deceived. I had often read of the smell of fear, but never knew what it was till then. It rose from our bodies and spread through the dusty darkness until it filled the whole cupboard. My mouth went dry. Ruskie and Fatime whimpered like puppies.

From *Only a Matter of Time* by Stewart Ross

## What good readers do

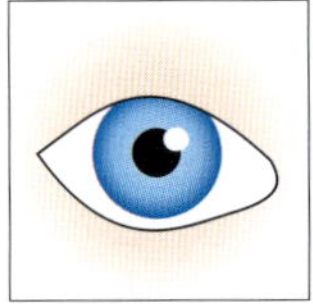

see images of the people and events described

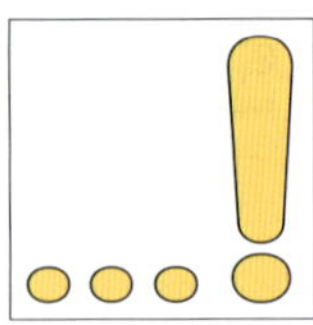

guess what will happen next

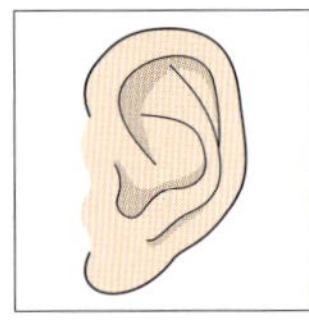

hear voices and noises, sense smells, colours and use their other senses

feel bored, get curious, feel excited, and sometimes let their attention wander

hear their own reading voice

reread the best parts and the difficult bits

remember similar events in their own lives

react to the characters and what they do

remember stories they have read before

put clues together and make guesses

ask questions about what's going on

feel emotions, feel for the characters

pass comments and make judgements – not all of them positive!

## Activity

1 Make a list of the things you remember thinking, seeing, hearing and doing as you read the extract on page 1.

2 Compare your list with other people's. How much was common and how much was personal? And how do you account for the similarities and differences in response?

## Examples of reading journals

Jane Eyre – Chapter One

Miserable setting in winter.
Miserable narrator – presumably Jane Eyre?
A lot about how cold, sad, raw it all is.

"She regretted to be under the necessity of keeping me at a distance" – did anyone ever speak like this? Sounds very formal.

— Can't work out who Bessie is.

"Shrined in double retirement" and so on. The language is dificult. Some bits are simple (eg how she was bullied) but the bits about conversations are hard to follow.

She fights back. But who is she? They are all called Reed and she is Eyre. A visitor? A cousin?

He looked around him fearfully. It was completely dark, there was nothing. But things moved, suddenly, there were off, dropping, rustling, scuttering noises, movements in the water. Twigs cracked.

Only Hooper slept, turning over and whimpering now and then.

Kingshaw wished he had a blanket to hide his head under. He could lie down and close his eyes until they ached, but it wouldn't be the same, because his skin felt exposed, and he had only to half-open the lids, to see into the darkness. A blanket would have muffled anything, made him feel safe. What ever came, then, he needn't know about it.

The woods crept and stirred. Kingshaw felt himself holding his breath. Every so often, he glanced round, over his shoulder. The fire cast shadows and odd flickers, into the darkness, occasionally it shifted, and the twigs collapsed into soft, ashy heaps.

*From I'm the King of the Castle by Susan Hill*

Strong sense of fear

darkness repeated

scary noises

## Keeping a record of key information as you read

Your English teacher will expect you to keep track of the plot and the characters when you read a novel. You can do this by filling in a simple grid after each chapter, like this:

| Chapter | Plot | Character 1 (Drita) | Character 2 (Zoran) |
|---|---|---|---|
| 1 | Drita returns home from school. Family meeting. War is approaching. She is forbidden to go to school because the journey is no longer safe. | • *teenage girl*<br>• *keen on school*<br>• *rebellious – argues back* | |
| 2 | Flashback to Drita's first meeting with boyfriend Zoran. He is Serbian, she is Albanian. They agree that the war is stupid, and quickly warm to each other. | • *speaks her mind*<br>• *confident*<br>• *soft-hearted*<br>• *falls for Zoran right away* | • *intelligent*<br>• *history student*<br>• *free thinker*<br>• *hates violence* |

Notes about *Only a Matter of Time* by Stewart Ross

Sometimes you are given other important information that you have to hold in your head when you read. If there's too much to remember, you can make a special note or diagram in your reading journal.

## Some useful note forms

### Family trees

Keep a note of relationships in **family trees**, such as this one from Shakespeare's play *Hamlet.*

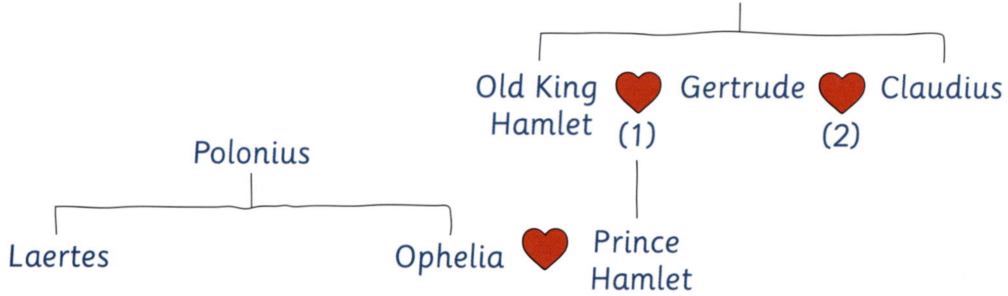

## Sketches of locations

Draw a sketch of what is described. Here is the stage set from the play *The Caretaker*.

## Timeline

Record the chain of events in a **flow chart**, like this one from Charles Dickens' novel *Oliver Twist.*

**CHAPTER 1** *Oliver born in workhouse*

↓

*Mother dies*

↓

**CHAPTER 2** *Moved to main workhouse*

↓

*Asks for more!*

↓

**CHAPTER 3** *Solitary confinement*

↓

*Nearly becomes a chimney sweep*

↓

**CHAPTER 4** *Becomes an undertaker's apprentice*

# Test it

Read the text. Take 10–15 minutes to read and note your responses on a clean sheet of paper.

## A cottage holiday

Our cottage couldn't have been more perfect. It was surrounded by beautiful country walks, was in sight of the sea, and stood in its own pretty garden where we picked blackcurrants from the bushes.

Inside, the stone flags on the floor of the kitchen, and the rough plastered walls, gave a homely feel. There was a well-appointed bathroom and kitchen, and central heating if you fancy a winter rent. The well-chosen furnishings achieved modern comfort while preserving the period mood.

The centre of social activity in Kirby Brade is, of course, the pub, where visitors find a warm welcome. But the winding lanes, the long stretches of almost deserted beach, and the patches of ancient woodland provide plenty of entertainment for those seeking a get-away-from-it-all break. There is a beautiful little church, dating from the fifteenth century, and the village even has its own quaint old English custom. Close beside the churchyard's north wall is a faint bump in the grass, pointed out to me by the Vicar. This was, he said, 'the black dog's grave' and local children put flowers on it. Indeed, as we leaned on the wall in the sun, there were a couple of roses lying on the grave.

From 'Padfoot' by Susan Price

## What you get marks for

| | |
|---|---|
| For visualising the village | 3 marks |
| For picking out several striking or thought-provoking details | 2 marks |
| For noticing any themes, storylines or angles which the writer seems to focus on | 2 marks |
| 1 mark each for any other type of responses listed on page 2 | 3 marks |
| **Total** | **10 marks** |

# Reading Strategies

## A2 Listening to voices in your head

In this masterclass you will learn how to:

- hear your own reading voice
- hear the narrator's voice
- hear the dialogue

### Hearing your own reading voice

Read this silently to yourself:

> The bus splashed to a halt halfway between the tyre factory and the tractor service station.
>
> 'Toskik village!' called out Bujar, reaching forward to take a cigarette from the crumpled packet on the dashboard. 'Anyone for Toskik?'
>
> I didn't need to reply. Every day old Bujar stopped his battered bus at exactly the same spot and asked without thinking if anyone was getting off. And every day he made the same remark: 'Oh, it's you, Miss Drita! So this is where you live, is it?'
>
> Picking up my school bag, I clattered down the metal steps and out into the cold afternoon air. The door hissed shut behind me.
>
> From *Only a Matter of Time* by Stewart Ross

### Activity

Discuss:

- How many different voices and sounds did you hear?
- What other sounds did you 'hear'?
- Was there expression in your 'voice', and how did you know where to put it?
- What help does the writer give you about how to express it?
- What helps to express it well?

## Hearing the narrator's voice

Narrators sometimes tell the reader all about themselves. More often though, readers work it out for themselves.

Narrators reveal themselves in:

- the opinions they express
- the language they use
- the things that concern and interest them
- the things they say about themselves

## Activity

1 Read the text on the opposite page.

2 Below are 12 statements about the narrator. Some of them are certain because we are told about them. Some are almost certain because you can work them out easily. Others are guesses based on the evidence. Which are which?

  **a** The narrator is a girl.

  **b** The narrator is American.

  **c** The narrator's parents are divorced.

  **d** The narrator is a teenager.

  **e** The narrator has her own bedroom.

  **f** The narrator has a caring father.

  **g** The narrator is in a temper.

  **h** The narrator is part of a reasonably well-off family.

  **i** The narrator is a confident person.

  **j** The narrator is called Phoebe.

  **k** The narrator has a pet.

  **l** The narrator can be stubborn.

3 For each statement that is 'worked out' rather than 'given', point out 2 clues.

## Giving up a pet

'Tomorrow morning I'll take Rocky away and you and I will go some place special.' My father tries to pat me on the shoulder.

I move away throwing pieces of twig on the ground.

Parents think they can bribe you into anything. Well, it's not true.

I pick up the flashlight and walk across the lawn, careful not to trip over the newly delivered firewood.

My father follows.

The banging noise continues.

Going in the front door of the house, I walk into the living room and look out at the Ashokan Reservoir. It's one of my favourite views, but tonight even that's not enough to calm me down. Nothing can.

I go to my bedroom, slam the door, and throw myself on the bed. I stare at the Sierra Club calendar that my father gave me and wonder how he can do this to Rocky if he cares so much about nature.

I'm never going to talk to him again.

There's knocking at my door. 'Phoebe. Let's talk. Or play Scrabble with me. You know you love to play Scrabble.'

DO NOT DISTURB says the sign that my father and I made up the time we worked out a system to allow each of us privacy. I open the door and put it on the outside knob, careful not to look at my father. Then I go back inside.

He yells, 'I'm sorry, but we've got to do this. Rocky's a nuisance.'

So are you, I think.

From *The Divorce Express* by Paula Danziger

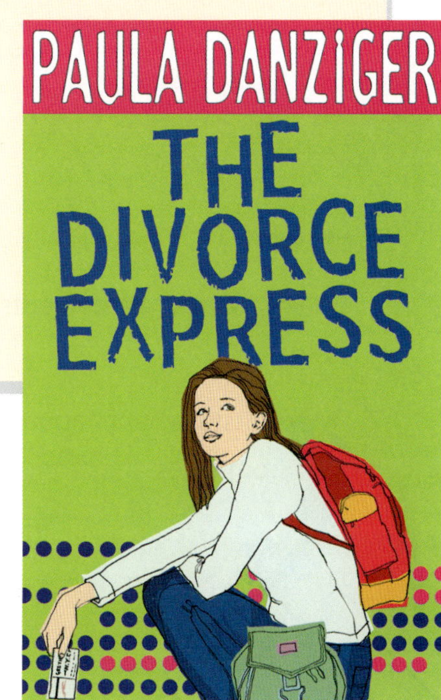

What can you tell about the next narrator from the way he expresses himself?

My name is Shawn McDaniel. My life is like one of those 'good news – bad news' jokes. Like, 'I've got some good news and some bad news – which do you wanna hear first?'

In the jokes, it's always the good news first, so here goes: I've spent my entire time on Earth, all fourteen (almost fifteen!) years I've been alive in Seattle. Seattle is actually a hundred times cooler than you could believe unless you lived here too. Some people gripe and moan about the rain and weather, but I love Seattle. I even like the rain.

I'm the youngest kid in our family, three years younger than my sister, Cindy, and two years younger than my brother, Paul, who, although I'd hate for them to know I admitted it, are pretty cool for a brother and sister.

Okay, that's the good news.

From *Stuck in Neutral* by Terry Trueman

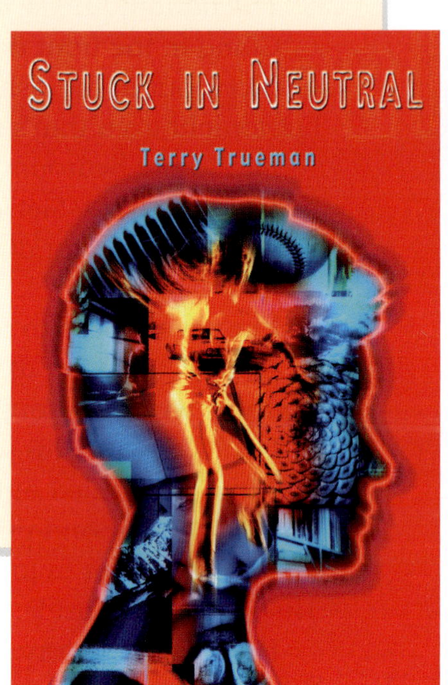


## Activity

**1** Make 5 certain statements about the narrator – facts you are told.

**2** Make 5 statements about the narrator that you have worked out from clues and from the voice he uses.

## Hearing dialogue

The best readers hear dialogue like a radio play in their head. The voices sound like the characters: they are the right age and gender, and they speak in a voice that fits with the words.

Read this and listen to the voice you hear when Grandma speaks:

> The door of his house flew open, and his grandma came out on the back porch. She was so old-fashioned that she'd fling a pan of used water out in the yard. She flung it on bald ground because she didn't have any flowers to water. You could see where there used to be gardens in her backyard and Aunt Fay's, too.
>
> 'Hooey, Willis Eugene!' she hollered out. She was a big old lady, big as Aunt Fay, with a hairnet on and a nightgown billowing around her. 'Get in here for your dinner, and I'm talking about right now.'
>
> From *Strays Like Us* by Richard Peck

## Activity

1 What kind of voice did you hear?

2 Can you see where the writer gives you instructions about the kind of voice to hear?

3 Do the words inside the speech marks make you read them in a particular way?

## Top Tip

### Reading dialogue

Glance ahead to the words just after the speech marks. It is there that writers give most clues about how the words are spoken. Look out for:

- adverbs that tell you how it is spoken, e.g. *gruffly, loudly*
- speech verbs, e.g. *whispered, yelled*
- punctuation marks, e.g. *question marks, exclamation marks*

## Test it

Read this and then answer the questions below.

Alice took a clean towel from the dresser drawer.

'Did something horrible happen this afternoon?' she asked, in her innocent way.

'No, why should it?'

'You just seem so—' she was going to say angry, but changed it – 'upset.'

'Why should I be *upset*? I took the bike out, that's all. Like I said.' He shut up his face to discourage her, but being Alice, she persisted.

'Did you meet that bloke you told me about, when you went back to the river today?'

*She* had a bike of her own – had she followed him? *Spied*? He wasn't going to put up with that! 'How do you know I went up there?' he demanded, glaring at her.

'You made wet footprints up the stairs, that's how.'

He jerked back to the sink. 'Quite a little Sherlock, aren't you?' he growled.

From *Scorched* by Josephine Poole

**1** Find 2 speech verbs that tell you that the boy is speaking angrily.

**2** Point out 2 ways that punctuation is used to suggest the same thing.

**3** Find 3 other clues that suggest the same thing.

**4** Work out 3 things about Alice's character from this dialogue.

### What you get marks for

| | |
|---|---|
| 2 speech verbs indicating anger | 2 marks |
| 2 punctuation or presentational devices indicating anger | 2 marks |
| Any 3 clues that indicate anger | 3 marks |
| 3 statements about Alice's character backed up with evidence from the text | 3 marks |
| **Total** | **10 marks** |

# Reading Strategies

## A3 Reading between the lines

In this masterclass you will learn how to:

- see how writers communicate directly and sometimes indirectly
- infer a meaning
- recognise the use of symbols

### Hints and clues

Writers do not tell us everything directly. Sometimes they let us work out what they mean.

He walked down the drive and across the road. It was getting dark, and a fine smirr of rain was blowing in from the sea. Mick wished he'd brought a jacket, but he wasn't going back now. He half closed his eyes against the dampness in the wind. Better out here than in the stuffy room with everyone smiling at each other.

He followed the familiar route across the green and rounded the corner by the pub, then crossed the railway line. The lighthouse beam was already flashing. It swept the sky behind the warehouse buildings, gave way to half-darkness then swept again, two seconds on, two seconds off.

I hate experience, Mick's mind said to him. He was fed up with the endless procession of things that kept on happening, dull and boring or else spiked with fear. He wouldn't care if it all stopped.

Quite suddenly he knew what he was going to do.

From *The Fortune Teller* by Alison Prince

### Activity

What can you work out about:

- the location, time of year and time of day?
- Mick's state of mind?

Writers leave room for readers to use their imaginations and to work things out for themselves. Some stories ask for more involvement than others.

Writers can:

- drop hints and clues in the details
- use symbols to represent the true state of affairs
- choose loaded words that influence the reader
- prompt the reader to guess and make connections

## Activity

1 Which of the above did you use to work out your answers about Mick?

2 In fact, Mick is suicidal. Now that you know this, go back and find ways in which the writer prepares you for it.

3 Can you find symbols that represent Mick's state of mind?

## Help

### Symbols

Symbols are objects or actions which are signs of the true state of affairs. For example,

- sunrise could be a symbol of new hope
- a candle going out could symbolise death
- clouds clearing can be a symbol of trouble coming to an end

## Making an inference

The writer offers you hints and clues. You put these together to make a good guess about what is happening. This is called making an inference. You have inferred that Mick is depressed, even suicidal.

Inferences are not always correct. They are just best guesses. To give a strong lead, writers sometimes offer several clues, each one confirming the others.

What can you infer about Mick's state of mind the next day?

> He barged into the kitchen with just enough time to change out of Jake's sweater into a clean sweatshirt and stick a fresh dressing on his burned leg. Cathie wanted to know why he'd gone off out last night without a word to anyone, but Mick just picked up his school bag and said, 'Can't stop now, I'll be late. I'll tell you about it after school, OK?'
>
> 'Well, OK,' said Cathie. And he gave her a quick kiss then went out.
>
> The clouds had blown away in the night, and the air was sharp and clear. The sea sparkled in the morning sun and gulls barked at each other in their raucous way, perching in the high lampposts to drop rude white sploshes on the pavement below. It was all very good.
>
> The school day was splendidly normal. Miss Armitage gave Mick a telling-off for not having done his Maths homework, but he dealt with it easily.
>
> From *The Fortune Teller* by Alison Prince

## Activity

1. Say how Mick's state of mind has changed.
2. How did you infer this?
3. Can you find symbols that represent Mick's new state of mind?

Inferences are often based on experience. Readers rely on their own knowledge of life and literature. For example, you know how certain stories tend to go. You know how people react to certain situations. You know how books often end.

## Activity

- What would you infer about the progress of a story containing these elements?

Midnight
A bat
An open window

A wedding
An ex-boyfriend
'Speak now or forever hold your peace'

Electrical disturbances
A small child
A radiant light outside the bedroom window

These are **stock events**. They occur in many stories on film or in a book. Other stock events include car chases, gun fights, punch-ups in a bar, and declaring love in public at the last possible moment.

There are also **stock plots**, such as:

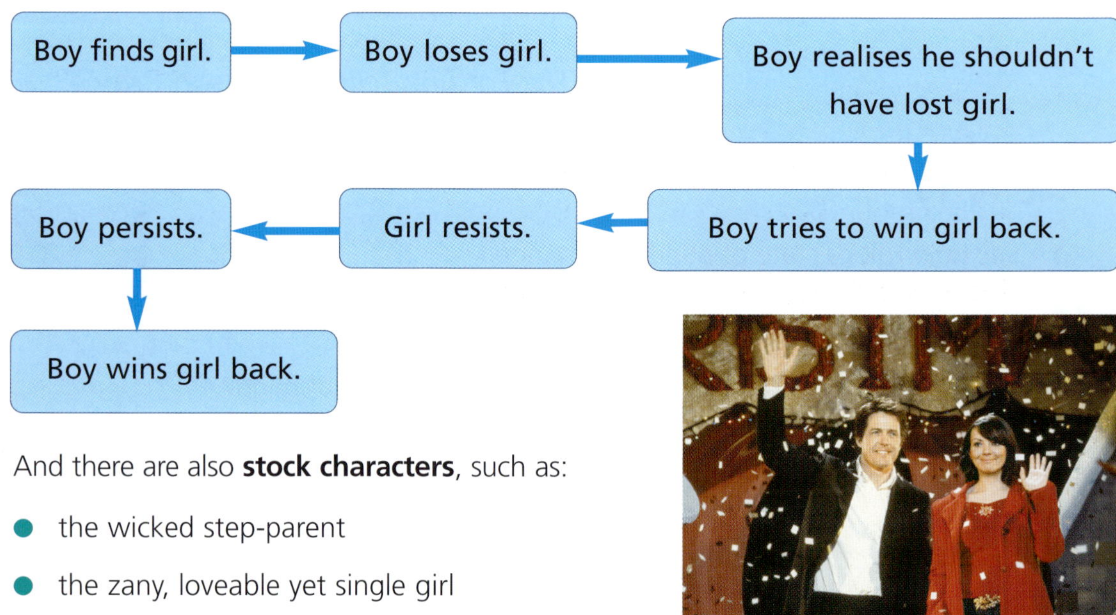


And there are also **stock characters**, such as:

- the wicked step-parent
- the zany, loveable yet single girl
- the insecure, loveable yet single man
- the incredibly intelligent psychopath who wants to take over the world

Can you think of any others?

Writers often use inference at the beginning of a story when they are trying to get the reader hooked. Gradually, as the story progresses, readers learn more and infer less. Most stories lead to greater insight and more certain understanding.

## Activity

- Read the following openings. For each one, say:
  1. What inferences you can draw about the setting, type of story and likely plot.
  2. How the writer tries to hook you in to the story.

His arms were stiff by his sides. His back was braced against the fur upon which he lay. There was no sound now. Even the whimpers of the children in the women's chambers, the sudden wail from the mother of Oslad, has ceased. Yet no-one slept. Hrethric knew that. All waited, their eyes open in the darkness; waiting. It was always so.

From *The Raven Waits* by June Oldham

Let's take a walk. It's night-time. It's cold – bitterly cold. Our breath rises up in front of our faces like smoke. Snow blankets the ground, frozen, twinkling; crunching under foot. The trunks of distant trees glow dimly by the light of our lantern, but beyond them is a deep and inky blackness.

The night crouches over us, held at bay only by our tiny light, ever ready to rush in and overwhelm us should the flame flicker and go out. A chill breeze plays among the winter trees, making the bare twigs twitch and whisper.

Something shrieks in the distance.

From *Witch Hunt* by Chris Priestley

## Test it

Read this and answer the questions below.

Mick sat down on the grass with his back against the sun-warmed bit of ruined wall, and stared out across the sea. You could see a lot of it from up here. It sparkled in the afternoon sun, and the outline of Broray was plain on the horizon. When it was wet or misty the island disappeared, and some people said it wasn't an island at all, just a cardboard cut-out that was there sometimes and sometimes not. Funny how they kept on cracking the same old joke. The sun was dazzling, and Mick closed his eyes.

*It's good up here*, he thought. No talking and anxiety, no guests to whom one must be polite. No blocked drains and draughty windows and leaky roofs, no frantic mother. The hill had been the same for thousands of years. Even before the Castle was built and fell down again, the rock beneath it had been here.

He stayed there all afternoon, but then the heat of the day began to pass, and Mick thought uneasily of his mother. She would be worrying. He put his arms around his knees and frowned as the usual thoughts started to creep back.

From *The Fortune Teller* by Alison Prince

**1** What can you infer about Mick's state of mind?

**2** Identify 4 clues which prompted you to infer this.

**3** Point to a symbol and explain it.

## What you get marks for

| | |
|---|---|
| 1 mark each for naming 3 different feelings or elements inside Mick | 3 marks |
| 1 mark each for clues in the vocabulary, setting, actions or descriptions that suggest Mick's state of mind | 3 marks |
| 1 mark for identifying a symbol, 2 marks for explaining what it represents, 1 further mark for explaining it clearly | 4 marks |
| **Total** | **10 marks** |

# SECTION B
# The Craft of the Writer

## B4 Ways with words

In this masterclass you will learn:

- how writers choose words for their effect
- to appreciate the qualities of sound, imagery and original meaning which are special to each word
- to recognise the connotation of words

### Choosing words

Writers choose their words carefully from a range of words that have similar meanings.

For example:

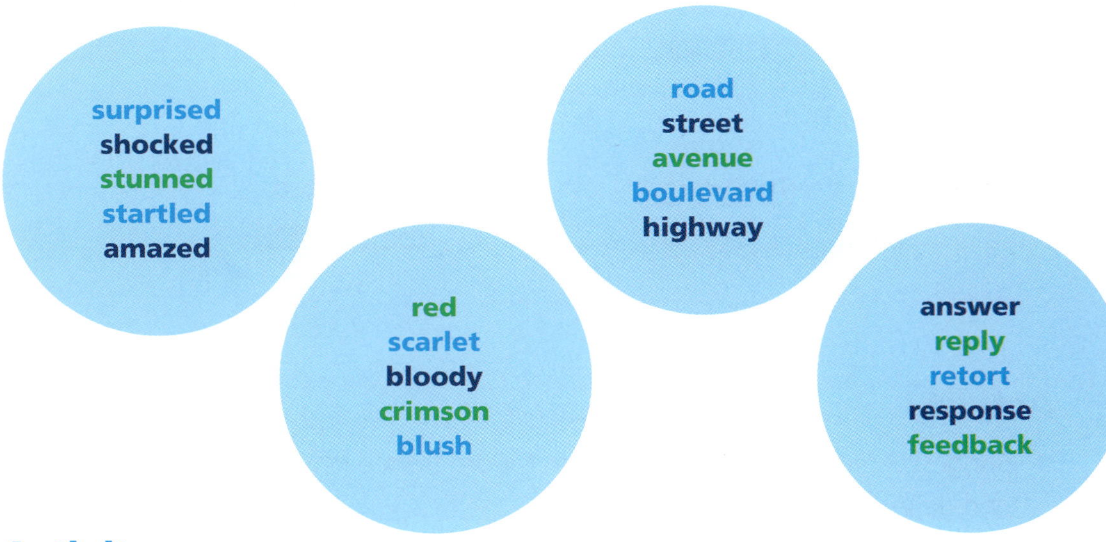


### Activity

Create word circles for:

- old
- house
- angry
- win
- shouted

So why do writers choose one word rather than another?
It might be because:

- it is the most precise word
- the word has connotations – overtones – which are useful
- the word has a sound that is effective where it is used
- the word fits the style

## Activity

- Look at each word circle. What is special about the underlined word? What qualities does it have that the other words do not?

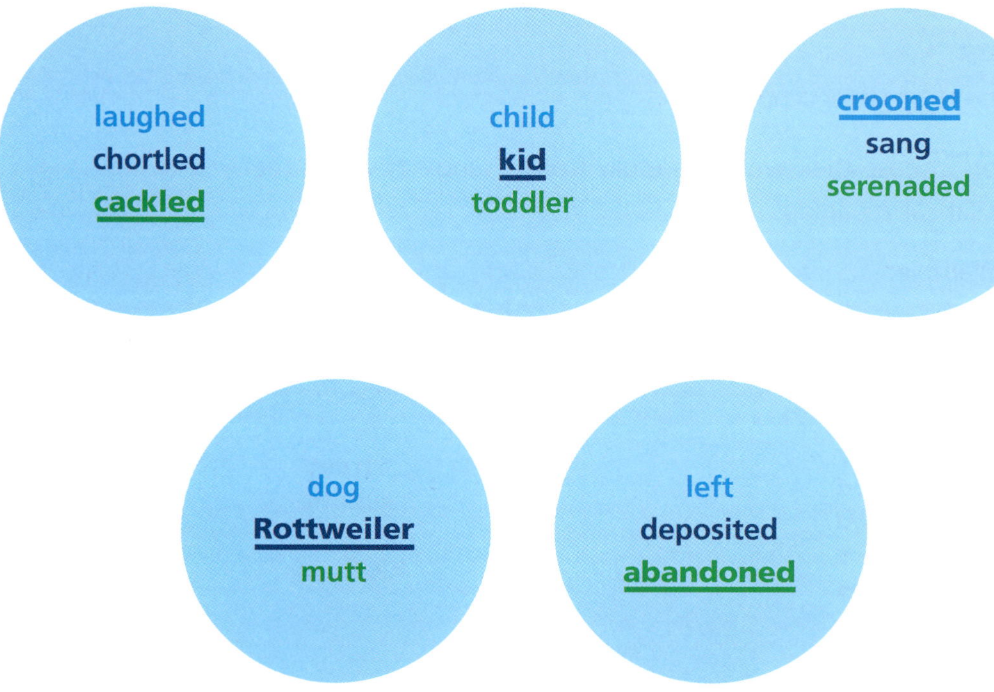


## Activity

- Suggest 3 more 3-word groups. Pick 1 word from each group and define its special qualities.

## Connotations

Connotations are the associations of a word. They are the thoughts, ideas and feelings that spring to mind when you hear a word. For example:

- red = danger, blood, stop
- gold = wealth, success
- oak = strength, maturity, dependability

### Activity

What connotations spring to mind for each of the following words?

- darkness
- green
- slither

## Words in context

Now see how writers choose and use words to fit in context.

### Entering a haunted house

Megan grasped the doorknob. It was embossed with a laughing face. She **twisted** it. The face went upside down and its expression changed from laughter to **despair** in a single turn. Like Brand, she thought and opened the door. 'Come on.'

She led the way down the dim corridor panelled in black wood and carpeted in **scarlet**. At the end of the corridor was another door, slightly open, with a **wedge** of light that coaxed a **tang** of woodsmoke and spices along with it.

From *The Ivy Crown* by Gill Vickery

### Activity

- Look at the 5 words in bold print. What other words might the writer have used here? Why might she have chosen these particular ones?

## The sound of words

All words have sound qualities but some words are onomatopoeic: they sound like the thing they describe. For example:

crackling
swoop
cuckoo
hush

## Activity

- Name 5 other words that sound like the thing they describe.

## The imagery of words

Words often come ready-packed with visual images such as colour, shade and size. For example:

a **grey**, damp day
Her face **lit** up
It **towered** over the village

Some 'images' refer to the other senses of touch, smell, taste or sound:

the **tang** of woodsmoke
a **bitter** blow
a **sharp** comment

And some words are used metaphorically. They describe one thing in terms of another:

The traffic **snaked** across the county
the **roar** of the traffic
He had a heart **of stone**

And sometimes this comparison is made plain with the use of a simile, usually featuring a comparative word such as *like* or *as*:

as cold as ice
a vice-like grip
a rind like that of a lemon

## The source of words

Some words have extra force because their origins sometimes come into play. At these moments, you can see their original meanings, their word family or smaller words buried within them.

He was **bewitched** by her.
They reached a **deadlock**.
She was a lover of **highbrow** music.

## Activity

1 Study the vocabulary used in this extract.

### Scared in the woods

Her heart **lurched**. All the warnings she'd ever heard about strangers **flooded** into her head: she was alone, in an isolated place.

Megan ducked behind the old tree and ran into the woods. She ran and ran, zigzagging **blindly** between the trees. She raced down a **hollow** filled with leaves, waded frantically through them, **scrabbled** up a slope on the other side. At the top she tripped, jumped up, **launched** herself away again, flying through the trees. She splashed through a patch of bog; mud **sucked** off a trainer. She stopped to try to pull it free, risked a look behind her.

Something moved in the undergrowth – a bird shot upwards, **screaming** in protest. She left the shoe and ran again further into the woods, deeper and deeper.

From *The Ivy Crown* by Gill Vickery

2 Comment on the qualities of each of the 8 bold words that make them especially useful in the text.

3 Pick out 2 more words from the text which strike you as having special qualities. Say what these qualities are.

# Test it

Read this text and answer the question below.

## Lost in the woods

Megan didn't notice the path narrowing until it disappeared altogether. Surprised, she stepped on to the grassy track taking its place and looked round. The river turned abruptly left, slanting noisily away over steep rocks glistening with wet moss and **trailing weed like drowning hair**.

She couldn't decide which way to go: by the river – which would be easy to follow without getting lost – or along the grassy pathway winding between the trees. Being **streetwise** was no good here.

She decided on the path between the trees, it was lighter than the way by the water.

After a while the path began to twist and turn, looping around clumps of trees. Undergrowth and bracken sprang up **clogging** the open spaces. The path petered out altogether. The forest had become a **wild** wood. None of the trees here were like the **well-mannered** limes and planes of her city home.

From *The Ivy Crown* by Gill Vickery

1 Comment on the value of each of the 5 expressions in bold.
Point out the special qualities that make them useful.

## What you get marks for

2 marks for each convincing explanation of their special qualities

**Total** **10 marks**

# The Craft of the Writer

## B5 Ways with sentences

In this masterclass you will learn:

- to understand agency
- to recognise whether a sentence is expressed passively or actively
- to see how a sentence is constructed and why

### Agency

The **agent** of a sentence is the person or thing that performs the action. Although the agent is often introduced at the beginning of a sentence, and is usually followed by the action, there is no rule about it. Sometimes the agent is not mentioned until later. For example:

She ran and ran.
*__She__ is the agent because she takes the action*

Her heart lurched.
*The __heart__ is the agent because it takes the action*

Coming towards her was a man.
*The __man__ is the agent because he takes the action*

Things as well as people can be agents. Things can be made to take on a life of their own, and this is useful for writers of mystery, horror and thrillers. You looked at the words below in the last masterclass. Now look at the way the sentences are expressed:

> After a while the path began to twist and turn, looping around clumps of trees. Undergrowth and bracken sprang up clogging the open spaces. The path petered out altogether. The forest had become a wild wood.
>
> From *The Ivy Crown* by Gill Vickery

## Activity

**1** Name the agent of each of the 4 sentences in the text on page 25.

**2** How does the writer use agency to create a sinister atmosphere?

## Shifting focus

The human eye shifts its focus from 1 image to another up to 2 or 3 times per second. In fiction, writers can shift focus, too. They jump from place to place, and in and out of the minds of the characters. They also skip over time.

Look at the way this writer moves between agents in the text below:

### A dangerous moment on the beach

He stood up and went out of the hut, shutting the door carefully behind him. The waves were pounding up over the shingle, pushing almost to his feet before they spilled over into a dying froth of bubbles.

Edward walked down the beach into the sea.

He held onto the breakwater. It was wet under his hand. He took one step forward, holding on, then another. The water foamed round his ankles. There was spray in his face. He moved on, slowly, deliberately; all the time creeping his hand further along the breakwater. Beneath him, the sliding shingle sucked at his trainers.

He couldn't move.

From *The Ice Boy* by Patricia Elliott

## Activity

**1** Make a list of 11 points, 1 for each sentence.

**2** Write 'Edward' against the sentences in which Edward is the agent. (You should find 6.)

**3** Write the agent of the other 5 sentences.

**4** What do you notice about the pattern of shifting between Edward and the other agents? This is a very common pattern in fiction. Why? Check your answers at the end of this masterclass.

## The passive and active voice

The **active voice** is the one where the subject of a sentence takes the action which affects the object of a sentence:

*the subject* → John welcomed Paul. ← *the object*

*the action* (welcomed)

The **passive voice** is when the sentence starts with the object and the action is represented as something done to it:

Paul was welcomed by John.

You can even leave out the agent:

Paul was welcomed.

The passive voice is useful to writers because:

- it puts the focus on the object rather than the subject
- it emphasises how people feel when they are on the receiving end
- the agent can be left out and remain a mystery

### Woken at night

Edward swum up through a deep pool of sleep and was aware that something had woken him. The night seemed silent; the sea too calm to hear. When he opened his eyes, the room was in darkness, but through the dark a darker shape moved soundlessly. It passed by the foot of his bed. The door was opened and a shaft of light from the landing sliced across the floorboards.

From *The Ice Boy* by Patricia Elliott

## Activity

The writer is trying to make us see Edward as vulnerable.

1 Find the only sentence in which Edward is the agent.

2 What is the effect of giving the agency of all the other sentences to someone or something other than Edward?

## Sentence construction

A simple sentence is a clause that tells the reader who did what. More *elaborate* sentences add in adjectives and adverbs. More *complex* sentences combine clauses and link them together to show how events are connected. These clauses are chunked up using commas. The commas help the eye to see the structure of the sentence.

Some sentences add on extra details for effect:

> A bank loomed in front of her, steep, covered in brambles.

Some sentences are hitched together with a colon or a semi-colon so the reader has to take them in together:

> She couldn't run up it; she had no breath left.

Some sentences start with adverbs in the form of single words or phrases which tell you something about how, when, why or how an action happened:

> **Abruptly** her legs folded.
> **In the corridor**, **from the open door of the bedroom opposite**, came the sound of someone singing.
> **Curious**, Megan paused in the doorway.

Some sentences contain details dropped into the middle of them:

> Cellos, **held upright by their scrolls**, stood in racks around the walls.

And some sentences take in several clauses so that you take in the bigger picture:

### Inside a music shop

He led them through a modest front sales room into a quiet annexe where cellos, held upright by their scrolls, stood in racks around the walls; violas hung in ranks; bows lined up on boards in neat rows.

From *The Ivy Crown* by Gill Vickery

## Sentence structure in context

### To the bonfire

Megan led the line of people along the sodden paths, past the river, over the grassy track. She smelled smoke, glimpsed a lick of orange and yellow. She reached the sweep of bracken.

'Light the fire,' she said.

He turned and touched the torch to the waiting timber. For a moment small flames played hide-and-seek in the lattice of wood, then, with a rush, they stretched out, surged upwards and roared away through the top. Fire filled the dancing ring with yellow light.

From *The Ivy Crown* by Gill Vickery

## Activity

1. Explain why the first sentence is separated into 3 sections. Why does this support the meaning?
2. Explain why the second sentence is presented as 1 sentence rather than 2.
3. How does the length and the number of short clauses reflect the meaning of the sixth sentence?

# Test it

Read the text and answer the question below.

## Swimmer in trouble

Someone was in the sea, not far out: a figure tossed up to the peak of a wave, then hidden in the trough. Again, a flash of white limbs in the sour yellow-green water, an arm raised. Was it a signal for help?

Edward stood where he was, paralysed. He couldn't take his eyes from the struggling figure. A wave engulfed it, then it reappeared, closer in. It was swimming strongly, making headway to the shore. Was it going to make it? Another peak, the wave toppled, and then in a shower of spray and little stones, the swimmer was swept onto the beach, almost at Edward's feet.

The swimmer lay there, gasping, face down on the stones. It was a man, in swimming trunks. His bare back heaved, gleaming with drops of water.

From *The Ice Boy* by Patricia Elliott

1 Find 2 examples in which the agent is a thing, not a person. Why does the writer choose to do this?

2 Find 2 examples of the passive voice, and say why this is used.

3 Comment on the way the sentences are constructed in the final paragraph. Explain the effect.

## What you get marks for

| | |
|---|---|
| 1 mark for each correct answer, 1 extra point for explaining convincingly why the writer chose a non-human agent | 3 marks |
| 1 mark for each correct answer, 1 extra point for a convincing explanation as to why the writer chose the passive voice | 3 marks |
| 2 marks for describing how the sentences are constructed, 2 marks for explaining the effect clearly | 4 marks |
| **Total** | **10 marks** |

## Answers

**1–3** Edward is the agent in sentences 1, 3, 4, 6, 9 and 11. The others are the waves (2), the breakwater (5), the water (7), the spray (8) and the shingle (10).

**4** The pattern moves between what the character sees, and how s(he) responds.

# The Craft of the Writer

## B6 How writers influence readers

In this masterclass you will learn how writers:

- load their words and choose details to influence you
- position the reader
- work on your emotions

### Vocabulary

Writers choose words to provoke a particular response in the reader.

> Mary stood waiting under a portrait of Sir Christopher Camperdowne, Sir Sidney's father. The canvas ___**a**___ over her in its ___**b**___ gilt frame, its dark background creating a ___**c**___ effect. Sir Christopher's hand rested on ___**d**___, which sat on a table in the foreground, beside a silver plate. He wore a long ___**e**___ gown with a sable collar over a rich red doublet, and a heavy chain of office hung around his neck. His face was ___**f**___ and gave the painting an ___**g**___ feel.
>
> From *Tread Softly* by Kate Pennington

### Activity

1 Choose 1 word from each group that makes you dislike Sir Christopher.

2 Choose 1 word from each group that makes you like him.

- a **1** hung **2** rose **3** loomed
- b **1** fine **2** heavy **3** ornate
- c **1** gloomy **2** subdued **3** nighttime
- d **1** a human skull **2** an archaeological find **3** an old bone
- e **1** white cotton **2** brown cloth **3** black velvet
- f **1** without emotion **2** severe **3** plain
- g **1** earnest **2** honest **3** eerie

3 Turn to the end of the masterclass to see the words chosen by the original author to present a *sinister* portrait.

## Activity

How does the writer below reassure you about this character?

> Kit came down the passage. She was middle-aged and middle-sized, and walked with her feet turned out which added to her purposeful appearance. Her hands were rather square, and she used them a lot when she spoke; she was a very alert sort of person, with nothing vague or arty-crafty about her. By far her most striking feature was her eyes. They were definitely green, such a deep green that they could look almost black; but when she was happy they shone and illuminated her whole face.
>
> From *Scorched* by Josephine Poole

1 Pick out some *descriptive details* which make her sound likeable.

2 Pick out some *specific words* which give you a positive feel about her.

3 How does the next writer make you share Anthony's dislike for his boarding house?

> Anthony's room at the boarding house was bare and unwelcoming. In the evenings he ran through Hyde Park, or skipped in the narrow backyard, until the perspiration streamed down his face, while his landlady, Mrs Pavi, cooked spaghetti and meatballs. He hated spaghetti, and would sit twirling the slippery coils around his fork.
>
> From *Daisy Chain Dream* by Joan O'Neill

4 Find at least 5 words that lead you to dislike the boarding house.

5 Find at least 2 details that reinforce this impression.

6 Could you tone down or replace any of the words to make the boarding house sound more pleasant without changing the facts? For example, *bare* (in line 1) could become *plain* or *uncluttered*.

## Positioning the reader

The writer positions the reader. The writer decides what the reader does and does not 'see', and influences their attitudes and responses.

Using the first person (writing as 'I') is one way of making the reader empathise with the narrator. To make sure the reader shares the narrator's experiences, writers will:

- let you see only what the narrator sees
- conceal facts that the narrator does not know
- tell you what the narrator is thinking
- tell you what the narrator is feeling

> At about eight o'clock, we heard a motorbike turn off the main road and begin the climb to the village. I was reminded of how Zoran had borrowed his cousin's motorbike to deliver his last letter to me. My stomach ached with the anguish of the memory.
>
> The motorbike came to a halt near the truck that blocked the road leading down to the church. The rider got off awkwardly and leant his machine against a wall. His face was blacked over and he was wearing the same military-style combat clothes as the rest of the gang.
>
> Wondering why he had come, I watched him talking to his colleagues. One of them pointed towards the captain and the messenger began walking round the edge of the village towards him.
>
> My heart gave a sudden jump. The young man's walk and build were all too familiar. It was Zoran.
>
> From *Only a Matter of Time* by Stewart Ross

## Activity

Find examples where:

- you are told what the narrator is feeling
- you are told what the narrator is thinking
- information is held back until the narrator gets it
- you see events from where the narrator is actually standing

## Working on the reader's emotions

Skilful writers know how to tap their readers' emotions. Most of us recognise feelings of guilt, sadness and frustration. These are the kind of everyday emotions that writers know they can depend on. Consider the emotions that are raised here:

> Her shoes rang hollow on the pavement. A dog barked in the distance, and the wind blew into her face. She pulled her coat around her and walked along Windsor Terrace. A light went on in the upstairs window of one of the houses, as an indifferent moon sailed high in a troubled sky.
>
> Dreading the thought of returning home, Karen decided to take the bus to Sallnoggin to see Betty Quinn.
>
> From *Daisy Chain Dream* by Joan O'Neill

## Activity

1 There is only 1 sentence in which you are told Karen's actual feelings. Where is it?

2 Look at each of the other 4 sentences. Say what feelings they provoke and how. Look for:

- choice of words
- symbols
- suggestive details

Advertisements also play on emotions. Advertisers know that people can be motivated to buy by guilt, anxiety, envy, greed or vanity.

## Activity

- To which emotions do these advertisements appeal?
- This advertisement says:

  It would make a great
  Christmas present.
  Particularly to yourself.

- This advertisement says:

  It's not your shoes.
  It's not your tie.
  It's not your car.
  It's your watch that
  says most about who you are.

# Test it

## Lost in a mountain snowstorm

The descent was terrifying. Between the clouds, the ground blizzard, and the flat, fading light, I couldn't tell snow from sky, nor whether a slope went up or down. I worried, with ample reason, that I might step blindly off the edge and end up at the bottom of the Witches Cauldron, a half-mile below. When I finally arrived on the frozen plain of the icecap, I found that my tracks had long since drifted over. I didn't have a clue how to locate the tent on the featureless glacial plateau. I skied in circles for an hour or so, hoping I'd get lucky and stumble across camp, until I put a foot into a small crevasse and realized I was acting like an idiot – that I should hunker down right where I was and wait out the storm.

From *The Devil's Thumb* by Jon Krakauer

1 Mention 3 emotions that the writer experiences during his climb down the mountain.

2 Point to 3 words or phrases that emphasise how lost he is.

3 Pick 2 details and explain how they are symbolic of his situation.

4 How does the writer make sure that you sympathise with his true-life experience?

## What you get marks for

| | |
|---|---|
| 1 mark for each of the 3 emotions mentioned in the text | 3 marks |
| 1 mark for each word or phrase which suggests how lost he is | 3 marks |
| A mark for each of the 2 symbols, and explaining them clearly | 2 marks |
| 1 mark each for naming 2 methods used to secure sympathy | 2 marks |
| **Total** | **10 marks** |

## Answers

### Portrait

***a*** 3 ***b*** 2 ***c*** 1 ***d*** 1 ***e*** 3 ***f*** 2 ***g*** 3

# SECTION C
# Finding What You Need

## C7 The organisation of texts

In this masterclass, you will learn about:

- how texts are organised
- the features of layout
- how the writer leads you through a text

### How texts are organised

Organisation refers to the way texts are chunked and sequenced. The chunking and sequencing depends on the type of text it is and what it is trying to say. There are two types of organisation:

- the organisation of the content into chunks of meaning
- the organisation of the words into chunks of space and use of visual signs

A **diary** is chunked into days and put into chronological order. There may well be paragraphs within a diary entry, each dwelling on a different topic or event.

A **newspaper article** contains chunks of information. These are often arranged in very short paragraphs within narrow columns. Each paragraph goes deeper into the information. It starts with points that will have most human interest, then goes on to further details and updates.

### Activity

Describe the organisation of:

- a recipe
- an encyclopedia
- television listings

## Features of layout

Layout is the way the text is arranged on the page and the way it makes use of space and signs. Layout helps readers to see at a glance how the text is organised, so they can find what they need quickly.

Visual devices include:

- *Headings and subheadings* – announcing the topic of each section
- *Paragraphs* – alerting you to shifts in time, topic, viewpoint or place
- *Illustrations* – giving you an instant image of things mentioned in the text

## Activity

1 What do the following devices tell you?
   - bullet points
   - a 'boxed' section
   - a change in the size and style of font
   - arrows
2 What other visual devices can you think of?
3 Identify the features of layout in the text opposite.
4 How does the layout help the reader?

## the main stage

**Take your seats in the jury for one of the most compelling courtroom dramas of all time…**

# BEYOND REASONABLE DOUBT

"Genuinely touching"
THE SUNDAY TELEGRAPH

"Wonderfully witty... superlative... most affecting" DAILY EXPRESS

### By Jeffrey Archer

**Directed by** Roger Redfarn
**Cast includes:** Simon Ward, Leslie Grantham & Alexandra Bastedo

**Beyond Reasonable Doubt:** In the Old Bailey, distinguished QC Sir David Metcalf is conducting the most important defence of his career - his own.

Accused of murdering his wife, Sir David finds himself locked in legal combat with his old arch enemy Anthony Blair Booth.

Step back in time to that fateful night, as the whole truth is revealed in this nail-biting thriller. You'll be on the edge of your seat as tensions build to an unexpected and shocking twist!

**TICKET PRICES**

| AREA CODE | TUE – FRI EVE | THUR MAT | SAT EVE & SAT MAT |
|---|---|---|---|
| A | 23.50 | 18.00 | 24.50 |
| B | 22.50 | 17.00 | 23.50 |
| C | 21.00 | 15.50 | 22.00 |
| D | 18.50 | 13.00 | 19.50 |
| E (BOXES FOR 4) | 94.00 | 72.00 | 98.00 |

**SUPPER + A SHOW**
**1st NIGHT** PRE SHOW + **FRI & SAT** POST SHOW

**DATES & PERFS**

**TUE 7 > SAT 11 JUNE**
TUE > THUR 7:45pm
FRI & SAT 8:00pm
MATS THUR & SAT 2:30pm

**FRIENDS DISCOUNTS**

**1ST NIGHT & FRI EVE** £5.00 OFF
**OTHER WEEKDAY PERFS** £3.50 OFF
**SAT MAT** – 2 FOR THE PRICE OF 1

18 **CONCESSIONS** AVAILABLE SEE PAGES **34 / 35**

GENERAL BOOKING **OPENS TUE 22 MARCH**

## Ways of organising meaning

### Help

**Organising principles**

- chronological (time) order
- alphabetical order
- order of importance
- order based on the reader's likely interests
- logical order, following cause and effect

### Activity

Here are topics for an article about common medical problems:

- measles
- mumps
- medicines
- home remedies
- visiting the doctor
- healthy eating and exercise
- colds
- flu
- coughs
- burns
- warts
- acne
- safety at home
- backache
- bruises
- precautions against infection
- first-aid kit
- sprained ankle
- hygiene
- cuts and grazes
- healthy eating

1. Group the topics into categories.
2. Decide on a sensible sequence for the categories.
3. Write a starter sentence to introduce each item so it links back or leads on from the last.
4. What different ways can you think of to arrange:
   - information about your family history?
   - an article about popular hobbies?

## How the writer leads you through a text

You have already seen how layout leads the reader's eye around the text to see how it is organised. The writer also uses words to lead the reader, by:

- opening each paragraph with a sentence that prepares the reader
- closing each paragraph by summarising and preparing for the next
- using connectives which show how parts are related to one another
- marking the passing of time or events by mentioning their progress, e.g. *that morning*, *before lunch*, *in the afternoon*, *later that day*
- repeating key ideas so you grasp them
- using headings

## Activity

- Which of these techniques listed above can you find in this text?

Grandmother was gentle, kind, silent, nearly blind and partly paralysed after a stroke, and that is all I know of her. The photograph I have of her as a young woman shows that she was beautiful. I sense that she was patient, loyal, non-combative and sad.

After visiting the grandparents, back we went to London.

The city was battered and bombed. The bomb sites were awful but exciting: full of Michaelmas daisies and nettles and ragwort and bay willow herb – and ankle-breaking rubble and dangerous walls which hadn't fallen down, and exposed staircases and rooms in which you could see wallpaper and fireplaces; and there were vast holes in the ground where houses had simply disappeared.

From *Out of India* by Jamila Gavin

# Test it

Read the text and answer the questions below.

The war wasn't over. By no means. We had no sooner arrived and gone to stay with my Aunty Molly in Streatham than the bombing started again. I know I was only three, but I'm not lying when I say I remember the siren going off, and all of us draped in blankets with pillow in hand, trooping out into the garden to descend into the Anderson shelter during an air raid. When we came out, all the windows in my aunt's house had been blown in. A house down the road got the full blast.

From *Out of India* by Jamila Gavin

1 What is the organising principle used by the writer?

2 Find 4 connecting words or phrases that guide you through the sequence of events.

3 How do the opening and ending of the paragraph help you to understand what the text is about?

4 How does the writer make sure you understand that she is describing a distant memory?

*And – not just about this text:*

5 Name 4 different ways of using layout to show how the text is organised.

## What you get marks for

| | |
|---|---|
| 2 marks for identifying the organising principle | 2 marks |
| Half a mark each for 4 connectives | 2 marks |
| 1 mark each for explaining how the beginning and ending of the paragraph help | 2 marks |
| 1 mark each for 2 ways the writer emphasises that this is a distant memory | 2 marks |
| Half a mark each for 4 ways a writer uses layout | 2 marks |
| **Total** | **10 marks** |

# Finding What You Need

## C8 Retrieval skills

In this masterclass you will learn how to:

- see at a glance what is covered in a page
- quickly find the parts you need
- assemble information in a form that is ready to use

### At a glance

When you look for information or ideas, you don't have time to read everything. This masterclass is about picking out ideas quickly.

### Activity

**1** When you look at a page, there is a way of taking it in without reading every word.

- If you only had 5 seconds to check out a page, where would you look to find what it is about?
- If you had a further 5 seconds, what would you spend it on?
- If you had yet another 5 seconds, how would you spend it?

**2** In a moment, you will turn over and try the exercise on a real page.

- Work in pairs. One of you counts up to 5 slowly. The other checks out the next page and then says what it is about. Take another 5 seconds to look and improve the answer. Then repeat until you have had 3 looks in all.
- Look at the page in your own time. How well did you get the idea of the page? And how did you do it?
- List the techniques you used to spot the key information. What helped?

# Oases

Oases are areas in a desert with water at or near the surface. Trees such as the date-palm can flourish in the desert if their roots can reach water. Desert soil is often quite fertile, and there is plenty of sunshine and warmth. Where there is water, farmers can grow lots of different crops. They can also grow several different crops during the year in the same field.

In an oasis, good land near water is kept for farming. Usually, the village is on land that is not so easily watered. The crops seem to be in layers. In the ground itself there may be crops like carrots; just above the ground there may be melons, wheat or other crops; then pomegranate bushes or fig trees, with dates higher up still.

▼ A pool formed by a natural spring in Egypt.

▲ From this clump of palm trees and houses which marks an oasis in the Sahara Desert, the desert sands stretch as far as the eye can see.

Nomads may visit an oasis to water their animals and to buy and sell in the market. The oasis is shady and cool after wandering in the desert.

An oasis does not have much rain. The water comes from far away, where it rains more than in a desert. It is carried to the oasis in layers of rock beneath the surface of the desert. In some oases there is a natural spring of water. In others, a well or borehole is needed to reach the water. With modern machinery, boreholes can reach water deep beneath the surface. New oases can be made for more farmland or for mines.

Oases can disappear. Some have been swallowed up by sand dunes which smother the trees and clog up the water supply. If the water supply runs dry, the land will become desert. This can happen if too much water is taken out of the soil which holds the water, or if less water soaks into this soil because water in the mountains is put to other uses. ■

See also
Deserts
Irrigation
Nomads
Palm trees
Sahara

## Help

### Taking in the page

The places to look for information are:

- the headings and subheadings
- the illustrations and their captions
- the first and last line of paragraphs
- any text which is in bold, e.g. key words
- any small boxes which summarise information

Move your eyes left to right, taking in 3 lines at a time. Look for the main idea in them (usually nouns). Pass over paragraphs that don't look relevant after the first line.

## Looking for relevant information

If you know what you are looking for, then you need a strategy for finding it. You can:

- look for key words or words that mean the same thing
- check the headings and pictures to see if they are relevant
- look in the index at the back

Information does not always appear in the words you expect, so keep an eye out for different ways of saying it. Sometimes your topic appears, but it is tucked away in the text because it isn't the writer's main point. This means that *skimming* – fast-reading over small chunks of text – is a better strategy.

## Activity

If you had been told to look at the page opposite for information about the following topics, what would you have done differently?

- desert crops
- modern irrigation (managing the water supply)

## Assembling information

To remember information, you will sometimes need to make notes. The three main tasks are:

- to find the main points
- to reduce them down to a few key words or phrases
- record them in a suitable form – one that is quick to create and will be easy to use later

## Activity

Your task is to make notes of the process of making paper.

1. Spend a few seconds taking in the page opposite.
2. Find the paragraphs which tell you how paper is made.
3. Check the illustration. Can it help?
4. Look at the 3 sentences of the first paragraph. Which ones are relevant?
5. What would be a good format for the notes?
6. Making paper is a complicated process. How can you check as you go that you have understood the process correctly?
7. Now draw your format and make your notes.

## Top Tips

### Making notes

- Don't copy whole sentences.
- Leave out the details.
- Leave out little words – go for the main nouns and verbs.
- Abbreviate, e.g. use 'v.' for 'very', 'P' for 'paper'.
- Write a 'title' instead of a sentence, and follow it up with any important information.

Paper

98

# Paper

Paper is made from plant fibres matted together to form a sheet. For hundreds of years fibres were obtained from pulped cotton and linen rags, but during the last century it was discovered that paper could be produced from wood pulp. Now most of our wood pulp comes from conifers such as pines, spruces and firs.

When the logs have reached the pulp-mill, the bark is stripped off them. They may then be ground between heavy rollers or 'cooked' with chemicals to break the wood into fibres. These fibres are made into a thin slush, by adding water. The mixture then passes through 'beaters' which fray the fibres so that they will readily mat together.

For every tonne of waste paper collected and reused, at least two trees are saved.

## The papermaking machine

The pulp of beaten and treated fibres next passes to the papermaking machine. When the slushy mixture arrives at the 'wet end' of the machine, it goes onto a fast moving belt of fine mesh. Some of the water drains away through the mesh, while still more is sucked off.

The remaining pulp, still about 80 per cent water, goes onto the rollers. These squeeze out even more water and press the fibres firmly together so that they form a sheet. The 'web' of paper is now strong enough to hold its own weight. It is led around a large number of heated rollers which continue to dry it. Finally the paper emerges in a huge roll.

There are hundreds of different types of paper, and many go through other processes. Some paper is moistened and passed through heated rollers which give it a glossy surface. Other papers are given coatings of china clay to make them into high-quality art and printing papers.

## Recycling paper

Millions of trees are cut down each year to make paper. But it is possible to make perfectly good paper from waste paper. When waste paper is soaked in water, it breaks down into its original fibres. These can be used over and over again. Many newspapers are made of recycled paper which has been de-inked and cleaned.

## Flashback: paper and papyrus

Paper was made in China about 1,900 years ago. The Arabs learnt the method from the Chinese in the 8th century and Muslims took the industry to Spain. Paper was made in Europe during the Middle Ages, but it was rare and expensive until the 19th century when wood pulp began to be used instead of cotton and linen.

In ancient Egypt, papyrus was made from the papyrus reed, a plant that still grows in the swamps of the Nile delta. Papyrus was prepared by laying strips of the reed side by side and crossing them with other strips. The papyrus was then soaked in the water of the Nile, to make the strips stick together. The sheet was hammered and left to dry in the sun, after which it was polished with ivory or a smooth shell.

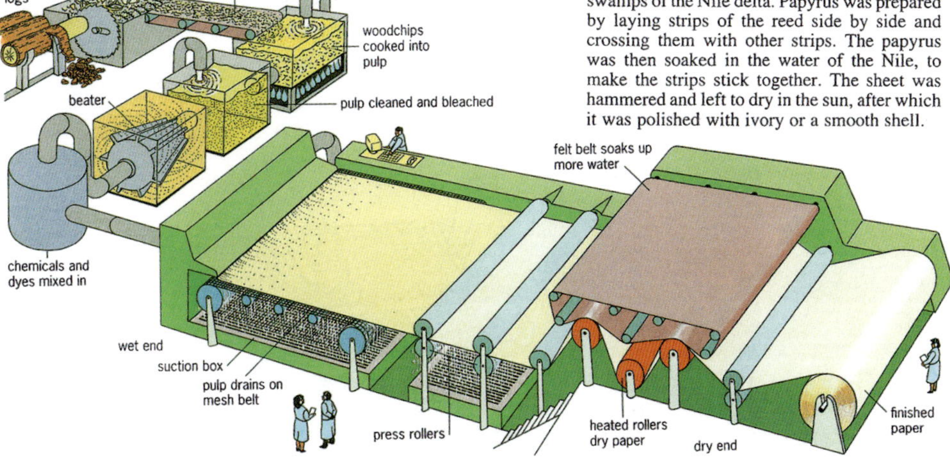


**▼ In a papermaking machine, liquid pulp is poured out onto a moving wire mesh. After pressing and drying, the fibres in the pulp form a continuous roll of paper.**

# Test it

This is a timed test task. You have just 8 minutes.

Read the text and make notes about how to make paper at home.

## Making paper at home

**Paper**
**Pa**pua New Guinea

### Making paper

To make pulp, tear up some scrap paper into small pieces and soak it overnight in warm water with a teaspoonful of washing detergent added. Next morning the mixture will be soft. To make sure the paper has really broken down, beat it with an egg whisk for one minute. If your mixture does not break up easily you may have to add more water or more paper scraps. When you have a suitable pulp, place four handfuls of pulp to a bowl of water (such as a washing-up bowl) and stir well.

You need a wooden frame with netting stretched across it and pinned to the underside. Use butter muslin or fine scrim.

Dip the frame into the pulp. When you lift it up, a layer of pulp will have settled on the netting. Let it drain, then turn the frame over and let the pulp drop onto a soft cloth or sheet of blotting paper. It will look like a thin pancake. This is your first piece of paper.

Place a second cloth or sheet of blotting paper over your paper and press out any surplus water by using a rolling pin. Repeat the process to make more sheets. When your paper is almost dry, gently separate it from the drying sheets and place it somewhere warm to harden. This will take about two days. ■

See also
Books
Fibres
Recycling
Wood



## What you get marks for

| | |
|---|---|
| For choosing a suitable, easy-to-read format for your notes | 2 marks |
| Half a mark for each of the 6 main steps noted | 3 marks |
| For reducing it down by cutting out small words and details | 2 marks |
| For notes that are clear enough for others to follow and use | 3 marks |
| **Total** | **10 marks** |

# Finding What You Need

## C9 Can you trust the writer?

In this masterclass you will learn:

- how far you can trust the writer
- to recognise the difference between fact, opinion, assertion and comment
- detect and deal with bias when you read

### Can you trust the writer?

You can *never* trust the writer. Writers can lie. They can conceal facts and they can present them in a way that influences your response. They can hoodwink you by writing in a style you think of as factual, but use it to sell their own opinions. Watch out for:

- **facts** – information that can be checked and proved
- **opinions** – views and beliefs held by the writer
- **assertions** – statements that sound like facts but are open to debate
- **comments** – neither facts nor opinions, but reflections or discussion points

For example:

> Research has shown that men are twice as likely as women to be serious gamblers. (*Fact*)
>
> Gambling is a type of addictive behaviour. (*Assertion*)
>
> Gambling is a vice. (*Opinion*)
>
> Many gamblers say that their habit started out as a bit of fun, but over time it developed into a form of comfort or thrill that they couldn't live without, like an addiction. (*Comment*)

## Activity

**1** Spot the 4 categories in each of these sets:

## Checklist

**A Divorce**

- ❑ Two out of five marriages in the UK ends in divorce.
- ❑ Three out of five married couples in the UK live happily ever after.
- ❑ Marriage, it seems, is a less-than-perfect fairy tale.
- ❑ Marriage is only for romantics.

**B Sweat**

- ❑ Everyone should use an anti-perspirant deodorant.
- ❑ Sweat is healthy.
- ❑ Sweating is a natural process that has become a social taboo in the west.
- ❑ A typical person has around 2.5 million sweat glands, and about 80% of them are in the armpits.

Facts from *XY: Toolkit for Life* by Matt Whyman

**2** List some of the signs that a writer is being accurate and truthful.

**3** List some of the warning signs of inaccuracy or bias.

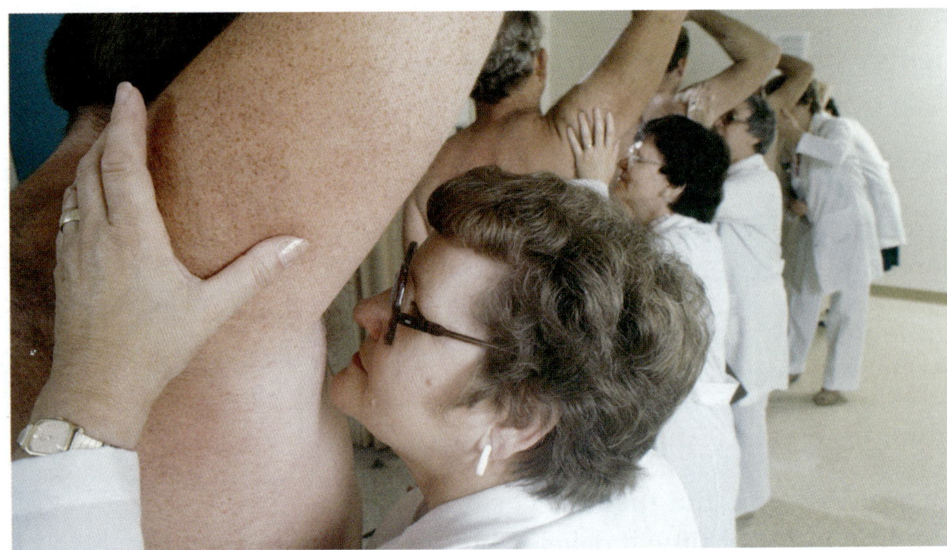

This article presents the arguments for and against the right to lifeboat help for people in danger on the sea:

# RESCUE RIGHTS ROW REOPENS

The death of two lifeboat crew during a rescue off the coast of Devon last month has reopened the row about 'rescue rights' at sea.

The two men died during a rescue at sea when inexperienced holidaymakers found themselves in difficulties during a storm. They had ignored warnings to stay ashore because of the approaching storm, and the rescue was complicated by mountainous seas. The holidaymakers were saved, but two lifeboatmen were swept into the sea. Their bodies were recovered the following day.

'People who set sail in stormy weather cannot expect other people to put their own lives at risk to save them,' says St Meg's mayor, Glyn Tredegar. He points to the 40% of rescues which are the result of human error and misadventure.

The Lifeboat Service is committed in its constitution to rescue any sailor in distress on the sea, no matter how he or she came to be in difficulties. But should they? Lifeboat officer John Crowne is clear that the service should stick to its principles: 'Once you start to pick and choose who to save and who to let die, you are in a moral fix. All life is precious, even if the sailor has made a bad decision.'

But Jane Butler, wife of one of the drowned crew members, sees it differently: 'It is one thing to rescue innocent lives at peril, but quite another to offer your own life to save someone who chose to ignore all warnings. Lifeboat crews cannot be expected to pay for other people's selfish and suicidal choices. People must realise that putting to sea is always a risk, and there are no guarantees.'

## Activity

- How does the writer avoid bias and personal opinion?

## Opinion and bias

Opinion is not a bad thing. The expression of strong beliefs, ideas and arguments is very important in a democracy. At the same time, you don't want to be taken in by every opinion you ever hear. You also need to guard against bias, when strongly held opinions lead writers to ignore or misrepresent other views.

Bias is often expressed in:

- exaggeration
- claims made without supporting examples or statistics
- the use of loaded or emotional language
- statements that can't be proved
- only mentioning things that support your own opinion
- keeping quiet about alternative views
- misrepresenting alternative views
- failing to mention exceptions
- passing off personal opinions as 'common sense'
- overuse of supporting phrases, e.g. 'obviously', 'certainly'

## Activity

- Spot the signs of bias in this text:

> Women make poor drivers because they lack confidence and swift responses. When traffic tails back, it is almost always a woman at the front of the queue, dithering about turning right or nervous about passing parked cars. It takes women twice as long to turn right as men; they just don't have the nerve for it. And flashing amber means nothing to them; only green will get them off the line. Heaven save us from women drivers.

## Being a critical reader

Be aware that writers can influence you. When you read, stay alert to their influence by:

- asking questions of the text, e.g. Is that really true?
- checking against your own common sense and experience, e.g. Have I found that the case?
- keeping an eye on words and phrases that lull you into agreement, e.g. 'obviously', 'always', 'never', 'as we all know', 'the fact is…'
- looking for the signs of honesty, e.g. evidence

## Activity

As you read this text, check if you trust it:

### Dress well

Dress well means exactly that – dress well. There is simply no excuse for dressing badly, dressing down, dressing dumb, dressing cheaply or dressing carelessly.

I'm afraid that this rule is very important and must be strictly adhered

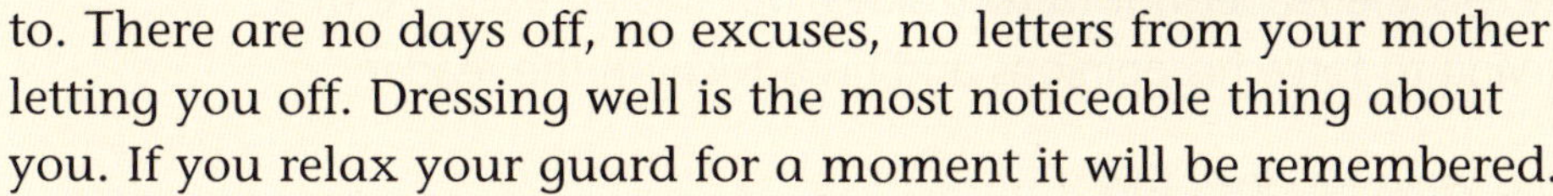

to. There are no days off, no excuses, no letters from your mother letting you off. Dressing well is the most noticeable thing about you. If you relax your guard for a moment it will be remembered.

From *The Rules of Work* by Richard Templar

1 What would you wish to question or check in the text?

2 How would you check?

# Test it

Read the text and answer the questions below.

## Don't take sides

If you take sides, then you are part of the argument, the fight, the dispute, the disagreement. You have to remain totally objective and firmly in the middle. Stay on the fence whatever you do, because if you don't, then one side will blame you as well as the person they were arguing with originally.

The more detached you appear to be, the more senior you will come across. If you jump in with your boots on and take sides, you run the risk of making an enemy as well as being seen as hot-headed.

The difficulty is when a friend is embroiled in a row with another less close colleague. Your friend will invariably turn to you and try to drag you in. 'Oh for God's sake, tell her I'm right will you, Richard?'

You can't afford to be dragged in. You will have to hold up your hands defensively and say, 'Don't involve me. If you two can't sort this out sensibly and without arguing I will send you to your room.'

From *The Rules of Work* by Richard Templar

The text tells the reader not to take sides, but it is an example of a writer trying to force his opinions and his advice on the reader.

1 Find 5 ways he does this.

2 Give an example of each.

3 Explain why the reader should not trust the writer.

## What you get marks for

| | |
|---|---|
| 1 mark for each way of forcing an opinion | 5 marks |
| Half a mark for each of the 5 examples | 2.5 marks |
| Half a mark for each explanation | 2.5 marks |
| **Total** | **10 marks** |

# SECTION D
# Literature

## D10 Character and motivation

In this masterclass you will learn:

- how to keep track of characters in a novel
- how characters' personalities are revealed
- to consider the motivation of characters

### Recording character

An easy way to record what you know about a character is to build up a picture of them as you read. There are 3 common methods of doing this:

**1** Note down the main features of their personality:

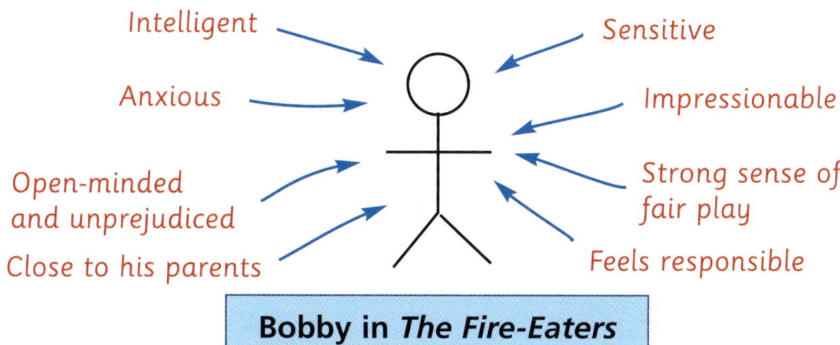


**2** Assemble a fact file of information about them:

**Fact file**

**BOBBY BURNS**

| | |
|---|---|
| **Age:** | 11 |
| **Born:** | 1952 |
| **Father:** | Fitter in shipyard |
| **Mother:** | Housewife |
| **Address:** | Keely Bay near Newcastle |
| **Religion:** | Catholic |

**3** Record their development and role in the plot as you read:

| Chapter | Plot | What is revealed about the character |
|---|---|---|
| 1 | Visits Newcastle with Mum<br>Sees the strongman | • impressionable – he is very struck by the strongman<br>• still young and rather insecure – often looks for reassurance from his mother |
| 2 | Visits market and takes lift to bridge | • observant – notices details of the shoreline |
| 3 | Journey home by train | • close to his mother – 'I let Mam put an arm round me', 'I tried to listen to her heart'<br>• observant – details of landscape glimpsed from train<br>• quiet – his mother says he is unusually quiet these days<br>• close family – Dad is waiting for them at bus stop 'she giggled and kissed him' |

## How you come to know a character

As a reader, you find out about characters in much the same way as you find out about real people. You see what they do and listen to what they say. In literature, you have the added help of the narrator, who sometimes tells you things about the character, or lets you into their thoughts and feelings so you know them 'from the inside'. Some writers also give their characters names and an appearance that signals their personalities, e.g. Mr Gradgrind in *Hard Times*.

Read the text and answer the questions about the character.

She asked me if she could come in, and I couldn't think of a polite way to refuse her. She walked down my hallway, hugging herself, and sat primly on the edge of a chair when I invited her to sit. She wasn't someone you would have noticed if she hadn't invited herself into your house. Her face was pleasant, but plain; her hair was brown and hung limply to her shoulders, with no style. Her clothes, too, were limp and drab: a navy-blue skirt that might have been part of an old school uniform, and a thin, pale-blue jumper with long sleeves and a round neck – the most boring kind of jumper you can find. And though she was quite young – probably no older than twenty – there was something slow and tired about her movements and manner, as if she was much older than she looked.

I asked her if she wanted a drink, and she said that a cup of tea would be lovely. I went into the kitchen to make it, leaving her alone, sitting on the very edge of her chair, her knees pressed together, and her body bent over her hands clasped in her lap.

From 'The Dreamer' by Susan Price

## Activity

1 Draw the visitor using the details in the text.

2 Pick out any repeated words about her.

3 Pick out any repeated ideas about her.

4 Sum up your own impression of the visitor.

5 How did you come to your conclusions? Did the narrator tell you? Or did you deduce it from what they said and did?

6 Later in the story, the narrator begins to wonder if the visitor is a ghost. Is there any hint of this in the description?

Read the text and answer the questions below about the characters.

I always loved teasing her.

Before we were married, I gave her a birthday present. I got one of those large boxes that baked beans come in by the gross, and I covered the ugly lettering with gold paper, and wrapped it in more pretty paper, with ribbon bows.

She must have spent twenty minutes admiring the box, looking at me with big eyes, and saying it was a pity to spoil it by opening it. I enjoyed every moment, every look, every sigh, every inane repetition – not only because she was pretty and I loved her, but because I knew what was coming.

After I'd encouraged her by untying one of the ribbons, she opened the box. Inside was a lot of tissue paper which she threw on the floor, and a smaller parcel wrapped in blue metallic paper.

She took this parcel on her lap and gave me another wide-eyed, blushing look. Ha,ha, I thought: wait till you open it. Inside the blue parcel was more wadding and another parcel, wrapped in silver paper. Inside that was another parcel, wrapped in shiny red paper, and inside that, another gold parcel.

You get the idea. After two more parcels had been unwrapped she began to say things like: 'It must be fragile to need so much wrapping!' and 'Good things come in small parcels.'

The parcels became very small. When she finally reached the last one, it held a gobstopper.

Her disappointment was tasty, and even more so her attempt to disguise it. Of course, she had been expecting something small and valuable – like a ring.

Well, I thought. That'll teach you to count your chickens.

She remembered her manners the instant the disappointment flickered across her face, and she smiled, bobbed her head and crammed the gobstopper into her mouth. 'Best birthday present I ever had! Just what I wanted!'

From 'Hiders Can Find' by Susan Price

## Activity

1 Draw 2 stick people – Him and Her. Write key words around them to describe each of their personalities.

2 Identify 2 or 3 points which you worked out for yourself rather than being told. Point to the clues in the text.

## Motivation

A **motive** is a reason – or reasons – for taking an action.

Motives are not always simple. For example, what was your motivation to attend school today, and how strong was it? What makes you do one homework before another? When did you stop seeing certain friends from your old school, and why? Even though these are simple everyday choices, we often have several motives, and sometimes it is not obvious, even to ourselves, what they are.

## Activity

Read the text and answer the questions about the characters.

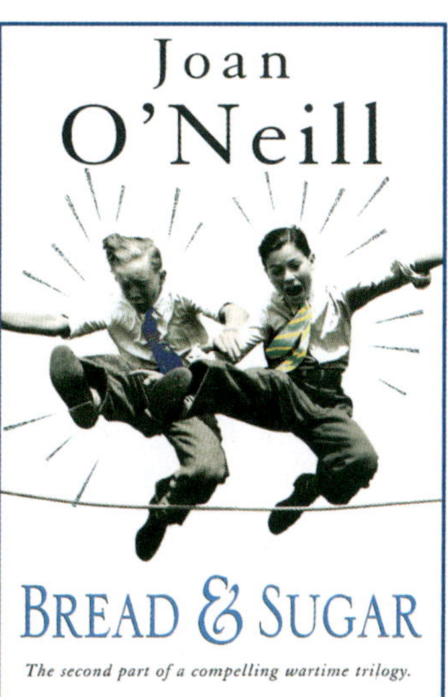


### Row with the cleaner

Mrs Keogh sang and clattered her bucket and mop as she worked around the house.

'Less of that noise,' Gran called out to her when she invaded her room with the new vacuum cleaner, twirling it around on the worn carpet.

'This room needs a good turn-out,' she began, lifting Gran's geraniums off the windowsill.

'Leave those alone. I'll see to them myself,' Gran protested, shielding the remaining pots with her outstretched arms.

'They're crawling with maggots. Look at the windowsill. It's rotten with the dirt. Look at the mould.'

'How dare you! I keep my room tidy. And I don't want you touchin' my things. I can never find anythin' when you've gone.'

'Calling me a thief are you?'

From *Bread and Sugar* by Joan O'Neill

You can see what they said. But what were they thinking?

1 Draw 2 stick people – Mrs Keogh and Gran. Surround them with thought bubbles that show what they are thinking.

2 The writer drops some clues about the causes of the bad feeling. Can you find them?

# Test it

Read the text and answer the questions below.

Biddy's house was a gloomy place; about a hundred years old, crouched at the end of a row of small terraced houses hidden behind the sea-front and the splendid facade of the Royal St George Yacht Club. The air was damp and chilly. They lived in the kitchen to keep warm. It had a stone floor, which Biddy swept regularly, a table and chairs, a rocking-chair by the fire, and a dresser with a few ornaments and plates on it. The other rooms were dark and cold. Her sister May imagined that they were people with ghosts in the dead of night.

Her mother had sad eyes and thin hair scraped back from her face, which gave her a severe look. Biddy thought her unreasonable when she shouted instructions at her, expecting her to carry them out without giving her any information.

One day soon after their father had left for good, May tripped and fell. 'God Almighty!' her mother shouted. 'Can I not turn my back for a minute?'

Biddy refused to let her mother make her cry. She would see that as a sign of weakness. Guiltily she ran to pick up May. 'Is your knee sore?' she asked, as she wiped away May's tears. She put her arms around her and held her tight. 'Don't cry. Don't cry.' Biddy rocked her little sister.

'Bit late.' Their mother gave Biddy a look of disgust.

From *Daisy Chain Dream* by Joan O'Neill

1 Why does the mother lose her temper when May trips?

2 Name 3 circumstances which may account for the mother's stress.

3 Give 3 reasons for having a negative impression of the mother.

4 What impression do you have of Biddy's personality, and why?

## What you get marks for

| | |
|---|---|
| 1 mark for each reason given for the mother losing her temper | Up to 2 marks |
| 1 mark for each circumstance that accounts for the mother's stress | Up to 3 marks |
| 1 mark for each negative detail | Up to 3 marks |
| 1 mark for each impression backed up by evidence | Up to 2 marks |
| **Total** | **10 marks** |

# Literature

## D11 Scene setting

In this masterclass you will learn:

- the role of the setting in a text
- the way mood and atmosphere are evoked
- how symbols are used to prime the reader

### Settings

Settings include:

- the location
- the time of day
- the weather
- the local atmosphere
- the historical period
- the social context

### Activity

1 What settings do you associate with:
   - vampire stories?
   - wizard fantasies?
   - fairy-tale princes and princesses?

2 What genres of fiction do you associate with:
   - violent crime in downtown Los Angeles?
   - murder in a genteel English village?
   - overcrowded and over-policed futuristic cities?

## The role of the setting

The setting has many roles. It establishes the story in time and place, and can be used to create a particular mood or contrast with the events. It can also tell us a good deal about the characters' lives. Sometimes it plays a part in the action. A sudden downpour, an avalanche, a riot or a labyrinth – all can be the main focus of the action.

## The setting as a backdrop

The setting is a backdrop to the events. It lends its mood to the events. Sometimes it gives the reader a familiar picture of where the events take place.

### Helping with a murder enquiry

Langdon could not help but feel a deep sense of loss at the curator's death. Tonight's meeting had been one Langdon was very much looking forward to, and he was disappointed when the curator had not turned up.

Again the image of the curator's body flashed in his mind. *Jacques Saunière did that to himself?* Langdon turned and looked out of the window, forcing the picture from his mind.

Outside, the city was just now winding down – street vendors wheeling carts of candied *amandes*, waiters carrying bags of garbage to the curb, a pair of late-night lovers cuddling to stay warm in a breeze scented with jasmine blossom. The Citroën navigated the chaos with authority, its dissonant two-tone siren parting the traffic like a knife.

From *The Da Vinci Code* by Dan Brown

## Activity

**1** Do you recognise this setting? How?

**2** Why has the writer of a murder story gone to such trouble to paint a detailed picture of the view from the car window?

## What settings convey

The setting can be used to give the reader a stronger sense of what is happening to the characters. It can be described in ways that show what is going on inside them.

### Trapped in an ice cave 1

I felt trapped and looked quickly around me for some break in the walls. There was none. Ice flashed light back from some hard blank walls, or else the beam was swallowed up by the impenetrable blackness of the holes on either side. The roof covered the crevasse to my right and fell down in frozen chaos to my left, a huge cavern blocking the open end of the crevasse from my view. I was in a huge cavern of snow and ice.

From *Touching the Void* by Joe Simpson

## Activity

- Pick out the words describing the *setting* that also communicate the *climber*'s sense of hopelessness.

## Atmosphere

Weather and environment have always been used by writers to create an atmosphere for their stories. Think of thunderstorms in horror movies, or snow as a sign of Christmas holidays.

## Activity

What mood do we commonly associate with:

- a grey, damp, drizzly day?
- a dark forest at night?
- a tempest with cracks of lightning?
- a dense, silent fog?
- a blustery windy day?
- a glorious sunset over green, rolling hills?

The setting can:

- tell you how the character is feeling inside
- tell you, the reader, how to feel
- form a contrast with the way the character is feeling

Consider the seaside setting in this description of a man looking for his lost daughter:

## Looking for Rosa

Black wind rushes past my ears. It's a rough night. Out there, beyond the pier, you can hear the sea chopping and slapping its big wet jaws. A swell that would be dangerous if you were in it. Grey clouds skidding and racing across the moon, drowning out the yellow of its light.

Rosa!

I call for her – I call out for my daughter. I call out so many times I quickly lose count as one minute of calling overlaps into the next. Every time I call, my voice is straightaway sucked in by the wind, and swallowed. My tears, too, sucked away. My hair whips all over my face and I use my free hand, the one not holding the lead, to pull it back.

Rosa!

From *Something Might Happen* by Julie Myerson

## Activity

1 What elements of the setting tell you how the man is feeling?

2 Find words and phrases that reveal his worst fears.

3 How does the writer make you feel that the weather is deliberately obstructing him?

## Symbols in the setting

Writers sometimes represent big ideas in symbols. These are images which stand for something else. For example, a crown represents royalty, a cross represents Christianity, a snowdrop represents the end of winter. Writers often weave symbols into their writing.

In this true-life story, a mountaineering accident on Mount Everest leaves the writer injured and alone, having fallen into a huge cavern of ice.

### Trapped in an ice cave 2

A slight breeze ran through the crevasse and I felt it on my cheek, a chill, deathly brush from somewhere deep below me. The light in the chamber was a strange mix of blue-grey shadows and dancing reflections from the ice walls surrounding me. Rocks embedded in the walls stood out starkly in the wet translucent ice. I rested at the base of the snow cone, absorbing the feel of the crevasse. For all its hushed cold menace, there was a feeling of sacredness about the chamber, with its magnificent vaulted crystal ceiling, its shadows facing into darkness beyond the great gateway formed by the ice bridge in the silent vault beyond.

From *Touching the Void* by Joe Simpson

## Activity

1 Find the symbols of death in the text.

2 Find the symbols of religion in the text.

3 What do we learn about the writer's state of mind from the description of the ice cave?

# Test it

Read the text and answer the questions below.

It was now the beginning of March, and each day grew lighter, brighter as the waking sun trickled its warming fingers across the city. Often, still, the chill wind whipped itself up and the icy rain dripped down bare necks, but these were the final weapons of winter. Now, bulbs began to spray their colours across the grassy spaces. A few fresh vegetables appeared in the haphazard filthy stalls that sprung up like weeds in the shadowed archways. Girls sold daffodils, their cheeks rose-red, their hair floating free, blown like meadow grasses. Spirits lifted.

Robbie threw himself into rebuilding their lives. Each day he worked hard, often with Essie at his side. They earned enough to buy Essie shoes.

From *Fleshmarket* by Nicola Morgan

1 How does the writer indicate that winter is coming to an end?

2 How does the writer show that spring is just starting?

3 How does the setting reflect the people in the text?

4 What is your general impression of the city? Where does this come from?

## What you get marks for

| | |
|---|---|
| Half a mark each for signs of winter | 1 mark |
| Half a mark each for signs of spring | 2.5 marks |
| For explaining the parallels with the flower girls (1 mark) and the family (2 marks) | 3 marks |
| For summing up a general impression of the city | 1.5 marks |
| For explaining how the impression is created | 2 marks |
| **Total** | **10 marks** |

# Literature

## D12 Literary non-fiction

In this masterclass you will learn:

- the different types of literary non-fiction
- the similarities and differences between literature and literary non-fiction
- how to approach the analysis of literary non-fiction

### What is literary non-fiction?

Literary non-fiction is factual writing or true-life experience which sets out to entertain or appeal in the same way as literature. It also has the qualities of literature. Style is part of its appeal. And, although it can be very informative, it sets out to interest the reader rather than being a reference text or a manual.

Literary non-fiction includes:

- travel writing
- autobiography and biography
- diaries, journals and memoirs of famous people
- books about historical periods, events or figures
- books about political issues or current affairs
- books about topics which have public appeal

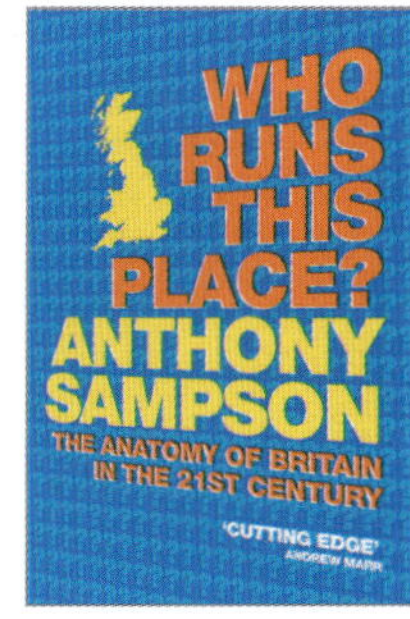

## The features of literary non-fiction

Readers of literary non-fiction tend to:

- treat the book like a good novel
- read it from start to finish rather than dipping in
- link their choice of book to a favourite pastime or interest, such as motor-racing, crime or politics

### Activity

1 Check around your class to see who reads non-fiction most and what type of non-fiction they read.

2 Most readers of literary non-fiction are male. Can you think of any reasons why this is the case?

### Activity

Read the snippets of text on the opposite page.

1 Can you say which of the snippets are fiction and which are non-fiction?

2 What features suggest fiction?

3 What features suggest non-fiction?

**A**

Catherine, kneeling by the table, lifted her mother's glass and looked at her mother, who nodded. So Catherine sipped at the wine, liking its warmth and trying not to shudder at the bite of the alcohol.

**B**

Battle lines in World War I were frequently drawn very close. During the Gallipoli campaign, the enemy forces were sometimes so near to each other that home-made bombs and grenades could be lobbed by hand into the opposing trenches.

**C**

They excavated the south side of the heap without finding anything of interest, except a field-mouse's nest in a tuft of grass growing up between some bricks. There were five babies, barely as large as a thumb-nail, shrimp-pink, blind and throbbing, perfect in every detail.

**D**

It was chaos. Three hours passed and we were still at this same point. I could not move. Every so often there were tugs at the rope which nearly pulled me into space. The pain of the rope and the cold made me feel faint. But if I collapsed it meant the end for everyone.

**E**

The stranger leaned still further forward, the neck stretching out, the head tilting sideways, so that the hair fell sideways, at first lock by lock, but then in a rush. Some of it fell across the face, obscuring the intent grey stare and the puckering mouth.

**F**

I wish I could tell you how I loathe this war. It is too horrible. The misery which it brings with it is altogether incredible. I begin now to dream of it all night, for it has become a terrible reality. Bad I always thought it, but I never dreamed it could be so bad.

## Help

### Features of literary non-fiction

The common features of literary non-fiction are:

- The narrator has a strong, personal voice and acts as an expert witness or guide.
- It is clear that the writer is talking about true events or information, and assumes that the reader is keen to know more about them.
- It is often – but not always – told in chronological order, like a novel.
- It uses the techniques of literature such as imagery, alliteration and powerful choice of words.
- It often offers vivid details, detailed descriptions and reflection. This helps the reader to relive events or to see what happened with the eyes of a first-hand witness.
- It is very aware of the reader and the need to interest them, explain things to them and draw them in.

## The style of non-fiction

Non-fiction uses style in the same way that fiction and poetry do. Factual writers try to make their information and experiences vivid for the reader, and they use the same techniques that are used in literature. Indeed, some non-fiction is so beautifully written that it is considered literature.

## Activity

- What literary techniques can you see in this non-fiction text?

I had no clear memory of the sequence of events on the previous day. Vague snatches of unconnected memory came to me – the hollow floor in the crevasse and the sunbeam, an avalanche blast in the storm, falling down the slope where I snow-holed, and that obscene ice cliff – but where had the rest of the day gone? Was this due to lack of food and water? Three days, no, two days and three nights! God almighty! The thought appalled me. I knew that at this height I needed to consume at least one and a half litres of fluid each day, just to combat the dehydration of altitude. I was running on empty.

From *Touching the Void* by Joe Simpson

## Help

### A checklist of literary effects

**Words**
- choice of words
- word association

**Imagery**
- use of visual images, metaphor or simile
- appeals to the senses of smell, touch, sound and taste

**Sound effects**
- use of onomatopoeia, alliteration and rhyme
- use of rhythm and pace

**Expression**
- narrator's voice and tone
- level of formality

**Sentences**
- length and structure
- active or passive voice

**Structure and organisation**
- way the text is chunked and sequenced
- how the focus shifts around

# Test it

Read the text and answer the question below.

## Mountain climbers take a break

We strung the tube tent as an awning,
lit the stove, and wrung our pulpy feet out,
sitting in the cloud, machine-gunned by water
drops from the great roofs that crashed out over
200 feet wide, a thousand feet above our heads.
We wriggled a little in the tent; slowly gulping
lumpy salami, a bit stunned, stuttering with cold.

At about four we took the hood off our heads and saw the valley for the first time in twenty hours: the curve of the railway line, the thin black line of the road, pastures of grass, the glitter of the river, the big stacks of corn like yellow firs. The red tractor a slow blood drop. Then we heard yells, names, my name, and saw a spot of orange jump at the toe of the scree. It was Lindy calling, calling and I called back.

From *Mirror, Mirror* by Ed Drummond

- This is a true account of a mountain climb. Point out 5 literary techniques which are used. Explain how they work and what effect they have.

## What you get marks for

| | |
|---|---|
| Half a mark for naming each of 5 literary techniques used | 2.5 marks |
| Half a mark for giving an example for each of the 5 techniques | 2.5 marks |
| Half a mark for saying what the intended effect is for each technique | 2.5 marks |
| Half a mark for explaining how each effect is achieved | 2.5 marks |
| **Total** | **10 marks** |

## Answers

### Features of literary non-fiction

**A** fiction, from *The Christmas Trees* by Susan Price
**B** non-fiction, from *World War I True Stories* by Clive Gifford
**C** fiction, from *The Ghost of Thomas Kempe* by Penelope Lively
**D** non-fiction, from *On The Heights* by Walter Bonatti
**E** fiction, from *Beautiful* by Susan Price
**F** non-fiction, by Robert Spence Watson (1870)

# SECTION E
# Analysis

## E13 Layers of meaning

In this masterclass you will learn how:

- to look beyond the literal meaning of the text
- to recognise the themes of a story
- to identify the philosophy and moral of the story

The events of a story are its **literal meaning**.

The **themes** of a story are the ideas explored in it, e.g. guilt, loss.

The **writer's philosophy** is the set of views or beliefs on which the story is based, and which it sometimes promotes.

The **moral** of the story is its message for the reader. It reads like an instruction to the reader about how to live their lives better.

### Example 1: Detective stories

#### Literal meaning

A crime has taken place. The police track down and arrest the criminal.

#### Themes

- Crime and punishment.
- Justice.

#### Philosophy

- Villains are clever, but the good guys are cleverer.
- Crime doesn't pay.

#### Moral

- Respect the law.

# Example 2: Lord of the Flies

## Literal meaning

*Lord of the Flies* is a famous novel about schoolboys who are stranded on a desert island following a plane crash. As time passes, the boys begin to change. They form tribes and new leaders emerge. They learn to hunt and find that they enjoy the kill. Gradually, they invent new rules for their little society. The strong boys take control and start to despise the weaker members of the group. The fight for survival forces them into a new way of living which is cruel and even bloodthirsty.

## Themes

- Man's cruelty to man.
- The survival instinct.
- The social order.

## Philosophy

- Human nature is basically that of a savage animal.
- Civilisation keeps our savage nature in check, but is quickly put aside under pressure.
- Relationships are really about the survival of the fittest.

## Moral

- Don't trust human nature in a crisis.

## Activity

Suggest the:

- literal meaning
- theme
- philosophy
- moral

of the following:

- a fairytale such as '*The Three Little Pigs and the Big Bad Wolf*'
- a soap opera such as a hospital drama
- a book, film or story that is well-known to your group

## Themes

Themes are ideas which recur in a story. The writer explores the themes through different characters and events.

Typical themes in **horror** stories are:

- the borderline between life and death
- curses
- science which oversteps the mark and runs out of control
- unquiet spirits

## Activity

1. What themes recur in a typical 'family' or 'street' soap opera? (Remember to look for big ideas rather than events.)
2. Are there themes in non-fiction, for example:
   - in the national news bulletin?
   - in a local newspaper?
   - in a history book?

   (Remember to look for big ideas rather than events.)

## Philosophy

The writer's philosophy is shown in the way the story goes and the way the writer treats the characters. For example, if the bad characters get their comeuppance, this is the writer showing that you can't get away with evil. If the events of the story are the result of fate or accident, this is the writer suggesting that life is cruel and maybe even godless. Common philosophies include the following beliefs:

- that good always triumphs over evil despite overwhelming odds
- that evil is always punished and good is rewarded
- that crime does not pay
- that suffering can make you a better person
- that goodness will win you love

## Activity

- Can you illustrate the philosophies above with common plot lines from TV, film or written stories?

## Morals

If you know *Aesop's Fables*, you will know what a moral is. Many of his fables end with a moral, which teaches the reader what they can learn from the story. For example:

### The Woman and the Hen

Every day, the hen laid an egg. Every day the woman sold the egg and made a good living. So one day, the woman decided to feed the hen twice as much grain so that the hen would lay two eggs and make more profit. But soon the hen became fat and lazy and laid no eggs at all.

**Moral:** Don't rely on statistics

## Activity

**1** Can you work out the moral of these 3 fables?

### The Monkey and the Camel

At a great meeting of all the animals in the world, the monkey performed a dance which delighted the audience and drew large applause. But the camel was jealous and he decided to do his own dance to upstage the monkey. But when he danced he was so clumsy that the other animals laughed and laughed.

### The Wolves and the Sheep

One day the wolves set out to make a peace treaty with the sheep. They told the sheep that there would be peace if only they would get rid of the barking dogs. The barking dogs, they said, were the cause of the problem. The sheep liked the idea of peace, and got rid of the dogs. But once the dogs had gone, the wolves turned on the sheep and began to eat them. Without the dogs to protect them, the sheep were at the mercy of the wolves. And, as you know, wolves have no mercy.

### The Boy and the Hazelnuts

Feeling hungry, the boy put his hand inside a bottle containing hazelnuts. He grabbed a handful but it was so full that he could not withdraw his hand. Every time he tried, his fist got stuck in the bottleneck. Luckily, a wise friend told him to drop the hazelnuts and start again, but this time to take a smaller amount. In this way, the boy was able to dip in, get a few hazelnuts each time and eat them all.

**2** Compare your answer with Aesop's original at the end of this masterclass.

# Test it

Read the story and answer the questions below.

## The inner man

Their marriage was a perfect union of trust and understanding. They shared everything – except his desk drawer, which through the years remained locked.

One day, curiosity overcame her. Prised open, there was – nothing.

'But why?' she asked, confused and ashamed.

'I needed a space of my own,' he replied sadly.

By Christine M. Banks

1 In 12 to 15 words, outline the literal meaning of the story.

2 Name 2 themes in the story.

3 What does the story reveal about the writer's philosophy?

4 What is the moral of the story?

## What you get marks for

| | |
|---|---|
| 1 mark for using between 12 and 15 words, 1 mark for keeping to the actual 'literal' events | 2 marks |
| 2 marks for each theme mentioned | 4 marks |
| 1 mark for stating the writer's philosophy, 1 mark for explaining how it is shown | 2 marks |
| 1 mark for stating the moral of the story, 1 mark for explaining why | 2 marks |
| **Total** | **10 marks** |

## Answers

### Aesop's morals

The Monkey and the Camel: *'Know your limits.'*
The Wolves and the Sheep: *'Don't give up your friends for an enemy.'*
The Boy and the Hazelnuts: *'Don't attempt too much at once.'*

# Analysis

## E14 Analysing effect

In this masterclass you will learn how to:

- describe your impressions and what gave rise to them
- explain how the writer creates a literary effect
- quote or refer to the text

Most tests of reading ask you to explain how the writer has used language to create an effect on the reader. A good way to start is to read the text and notice how it affects *you.* You will get good marks if you are able to explain how the writer did this to you.

For example, what impression do you get of this house?

It's no use knocking at the front door, because Mick won't hear, and the door won't open anyway. You have to go round the back and in by the kitchen door. It opens into a low passage that smells thickly and warmly of old cooking, old newspapers, and old tobacco smoke. Just inside the door a flight of narrow steep stairs made of old, worn, black wood, lead up to the first floor. There's a landing half-way up, in the corner of the stairs, and a little landing window lets a smudge of light into the fuggy darkness.

The windows are all tiny, and the door's so small that even I have to duck, and I'm not tall. Inside the ceilings are low, and when I'm in there I always walk about with my hand on top of my head, because I've banged my head on the roof beams and door lintels so often. The floorboards are always tripping you up, too, because they're twisted and risen. It's a wonderful house to visit, but not, I think, to live in. The rooms are small and badly lit, and at night most of the house is in pitch-darkness because there's no electricity. Mick never got round to having electricity put in.

From 'The Landing Window' by Susan Price

## Activity

What words would you choose to describe the house? Look at the words below and put them into 4 groups, depending on how well they capture the feel of the house:

1 right

2 roughly right

3 not quite right

4 wrong

| | | | |
|---|---|---|---|
| Old | Scary | Unsettling | Dilapidated |
| Neglected | Uninhabited | Spooky | Old-fashioned |
| Suffocating | Dreary | Miserable | Desolate |
| Unkept | Ruined | Tumbledown | Shabby |
| Seedy | Hazardous | Depressing | Oppressive |
| Stifling | Low | Obstructive | Dirty |
| Small | Quaint | Cramped | Untidy |
| Dim | Uncomfortable | Deserted | Unwelcoming |

## Explaining effects

### Step 1: Notice and name your impressions

Think about:

- what you 'see'
- what you feel or sense about the place
- what you are told

Then write down some words that capture your overall impressions of the house. The best words are specific and evocative. They capture the feeling well.

### Step 2: Look for the details which gave rise to your impressions

Now look back at the text for the hints, words or details which gave rise to your impressions. For example:

[box] = *house resists visitors*

(circle) = *atmosphere is oppressive, cramped, dark, smelly*

> It's no use knocking at the front door, because Mick won't hear, and the door won't open anyway. You have to go round the back and in by the kitchen door. It opens into a low passage that smells thickly and warmly of old cooking, old newspapers, and old tobacco smoke. Just inside the door a flight of narrow steep stairs made of old, worn, black wood, lead up to the first floor. There's a landing half way up, in the corner of the stairs, and a little landing window lets a smudge of light into the fuggy darkness.

—— = *repetition of 'old' emphasises age*

~~~ = *dark & hard to see*

### Activity

- Now search for hints and clues in paragraph 2 of the extract on page 79. Annotate it in the same way as paragraph 1 above.
~~~

## Step 3: Explain how the writer created the effect

To explain how the effect has been achieved, you need to spell out the main impressions and how they have been achieved. This means you must point to the use of language and technique.

**Example:**

The writer has presented a house in an advanced state of neglect.

Although it is lived-in, we are told several times that it is 'old', dim, 'worn' and cramped. The atmosphere is oppressive, not only because it is dark but because it is full of stifling smells:

> 'a low passage that smells thickly and warmly of old cooking, old newspapers, and old tobacco smoke'

The house is also hazardous: the narrator trips on the floorboards, bangs his head on the ceiling and the poor light will not let him see the inside. It is as though the house is obstructing his visit.

We never meet the inhabitant, and although we are told he is there, and we can even smell his presence, it feels as if the house is deserted. This tension between its stifling smells of living and the state of decay has an unsettling effect on the reader.

## How to quote

Drop in a **longer quotation** if:

- it sums up a point better than you can
- it speaks for itself
- it isn't too long

### Help

**How to present a longer quotation**

- Lead into the quotation with a short sentence to get the reader ready.
- Leave a line before and after the quote.
- Indent the quotation.
- Wrap the quotation in quotation marks: 'xxx'.

Often it is more effective if you weave quotations into your own sentences. **Quote as you go** if:

- the quotation is pithy and apt
- the wording is significant
- the author's turn of phrase is better than yours
- you can find a way to fit it into your sentence

## Help

### Quoting as you go

- Keep the quotation short.
- Put quotation marks around the words lifted from the text.
- Weave them into the wording of the sentence.
- Get the wording of the sentence right for slotting them in.

## Referring to the text

Referring to the text means pointing out evidence in your own words. Refer to the text if:

- it's easier to make the point in your own words
- the section you refer to is too long to quote
- the actual words are not significant

## Help

- **Refer** if the focus is on events, plot, motives, abstract ideas or summing up.
- **Quote as you go** if the focus is on choice of language, detail or literary technique.
- **Quote** 1 or 2 sentences only if they are good enough and important enough to merit a whole section of their own.

## Activity

- In the text on page 82 identify the 3 types of evidence.

## Test it

Here the farm is described from the outside. Your test task is to say what impression of the farm is given and how the writer has created it.

The house looks every year of its age. The roof's covered with dark, blue-black tiles, and grown all over with blotches of yellow and orange lichen, and big cushions of long, bright-green moss. It even has some tufts of grass and flowers growing on the roof, where soil and seeds have lodged in cracks. The whole roof ripples up and down – up where the tiles go over the wooden roof beams, and down where there are no beams and the tiles are collapsing. The roof's holed, too, at one end: the rain falls in the bedroom where Mick's mum and dad used to sleep.

At the back of the house is an untidy yard. Piled up seed boxes have slithered down in avalanches; broken flowerpots and broken tools have been thrown in amongst them and on top of them. There are piles of old newspapers, swelling and softening in the rain, and hamburger boxes and plastic rubbish bags. Weeds have grown up through all of it, long, thin, unhealthy weeds. There's a path through all of this rubbish to the old pigsty.

There's nothing in the pigsty except more rubbish now; Mick stopped keeping pigs years ago. But he likes to go out and sit on the pigsty wall because there's a wonderful view of the valley below the farm. You can see the whole district for miles around: roads, television masts, canals, cooling-towers, factories, houses, railways, flats, parks, power-stations. It looks best at night, when it's all lit up. Then the blocks of flats are towers of lights like the masts of giant ships sailing by.

From 'The Landing Window' by Susan Price

### What you get marks for

| | |
|---|---|
| For finding strong, specific words to describe the overall impression that is given | 2 marks |
| For pinpointing at least 4 ways that impression is created | 4 marks |
| For backing up each impression with evidence that is properly quoted or properly referred to | 4 marks |
| **Total** | **10 marks** |

# Analysis

## E15 Considering context

In this masterclass you will learn to consider:

- the historical and social background of a book
- what conclusions you can draw about the author when you read a text
- how far context influences your reading of a book

### Historical context

The context of a book is its social and historical background.

Some books are *about* history. But books are also *part of* history. Fiction books are important historical documents because they reveal the thoughts, feelings, interests and imagination of the age in which they were written. No writer lives outside society: their books express the spirit of the age in which they lived.

**Charles Dickens** wrote about the poverty and injustices of the Victorian period in which he lived. His stories deal with criminal gangs, the workhouse and the greed of the rich. He showed his middle-class readers what life was like outside their comfortable world.

**Jane Austen** wrote about the everyday concerns of women in the late 1700s. Women at that time were not generally allowed to own money or property of their own. Their futures depended on making a good marriage to someone with an income. Therefore, it is no wonder that Jane Austen's books are romances that end in a happy, wealthy marriage.

**Thomas Hardy** wrote at the end of the 19th century and the beginning of the 20th century. He produced stories about farmers, agricultural traders and farm workers. He wrote in detail about their way of life and customs. But Hardy was describing a way of life that was already over when he began writing. His books were a way of preserving a little part of the past.

**H. G. Wells** wrote science fiction in the 1890s. He described a future of science, machines, invention and exploration. It was fantasy, but it does tell us something about the fears of the late Victorians. They lived through a period of rapid technological change and wondered where it would all lead.

## Activity

1 Can you think of other writers and how they reflect the historical and social period in which they were writing?

2 Look at today's television listings. If a student looked at them in 500 years, what conclusions might he or she draw about the things that intrigue and interest us today?

## Does context matter?

When you read a story, you get lost inside it. You go along with the writer and accept the world of the story. But there is a part of you that stays outside of the story. This is the part of you that knows about the writer and the historical background and takes it into account.

Read this text and then answer the questions below.

> Someone must have been telling lies about Joseph K., because for without having done anything wrong he was arrested one fine morning. His landlady's cook, who always brought him his breakfast at eight o'clock, failed to appear on this occasion. That had never happened before. K. waited for a little while longer, watching from his pillow the old lady opposite, who seemed to be peering at him with curiosity unusual even for her, but then, feeling both put out and hungry, he rang the bell. At once there was a knock at the door and a man entered whom he had never seen before in the house.

## Activity

**1** Decide what difference it would make to your reading if you knew for certain that:

- **a** it is a true story
- **b** it is a translation from another language
- **c** it is meant to be a parable about modern life
- **d** the book was banned for more than 15 years
- **e** the writer was deeply depressed and emotionally unstable
- **f** it was written during a period of fascism
- **g** it was the last thing the writer ever wrote
- **h** the book won an international prize

**2** Only 5 of the statements are true for the text above. Work out which ones they are, and consider how you knew. Find the answers at the end of this masterclass.

**3** When you know the answer, does it cast new light on the text?

## Authors

For centuries, the only people who were taught to read and write were boys from rich families. When they grew up and wrote their own books, they wrote about the world as they saw it. Older literature tells us about the life and views of the most privileged people.

It is only in the last 100 years or so that education has given everyone the chance to read and write. More and more modern authors express the concerns and experiences of women, of the working class and of different ethnic groups.

These new writers have to find their own voice and their own style. The old ways of writing cannot always express their very different experience of life.

## Activity

**1** Read these extracts from autobiographies. See if you can work out which ones were written by:

- an Irishman
- a working-class man from the north of England
- a female Londoner

**A**

Gradually I got used to the commuting, even getting a job at Woolworth's in Shepherd's Bush after school. To my astonishment, I was asked to take an intelligence test to be a shop assistant, hilarious really, as I was studying for eight O-levels, including pure and applied mathematics. The text seemed to involve adding up the cost of a lot of light bulbs and pairs of woollen socks and subtracting them from a ten pound note. Luckily I passed with flying colours and was issued a pale green nylon overall. I looked demented in it, standing by the till behind the sock counter.

**B**

Although I had left school against the advice of my teachers I had, without telling anyone, tried to continue my studies in literature at night school. It was a tedious walk from one end of the city to the other every Tuesday night, and to sit amongst adults studying for 'O' levels was confusing. I was the youngest in the class, so the companionship that I knew at school was absent here. I stuck it for a short period. It was too long a walk on cold winter's nights, and then to try to concentrate on Shakespeare with wet shoes and soaking clothes, wondering how I was going to get home when the buses stopped.

**C**

There was only one good thing about going to the Co-op and that was the red notebook with the Danger Don'ts on the back that my Aunt Betty used to write the orders down in. She wrote everything down on a fresh page every week, and the Co-op man, he used to cross each thing out as he put it in the basket. Then he would tear off a piece of that paper that they put yeast in and wrap the change up in it. Never gave *me* anything, though. Anyway, what I used to do with this notebook, every week I used to pinch four blank pages out of the middle.

2 Identify which author wrote which text. Then check your answers at the end of this masterclass.

3 What clues in the **content** led you to identify the correct author?

4 What clues in the **style** led you to identify the correct author?

5 Was there anything in the **attitude** of the writer that helped you to identify the correct author?

- Many modern writers adopt a style which reflects their natural voice and rhythms of thought. The best insight into the writer is gained from the values, themes and philosophy expressed in the text.

# Test it

Read the text and answer the questions below.

I returned from the City about three o'clock on that May afternoon pretty well disgusted with life. I had been three months in the Old Country, and was fed up with it. If anyone had told me a year ago that I would have been feeling like that I should have laughed at him; but there was the fact. The weather made me liverish, the talk of the ordinary Englishman made me sick. I couldn't get enough exercise, and the amusements of London seemed as flat as soda-water that has been standing in the sun.

About six o'clock I went home, dressed, dined at the Café Royal, and turned into a music hall. It was a silly show, all capering women and monkey-faced men, and I did not stay long. The night was fine and clear as I walked back to the flat I had hired near Portland Place. The crowd surged past me on the pavements, busy and chattering, and I envied the people for having something to do. These shop-girls and clerks and dandies and policemen had some interest in life that kept them going.

**1** The text was written in 1914. Find and explain 4 details that confirm this period in history.

**2** Do you think the text was written by a man or a woman? Give 3 reasons.

**3** What light would it cast on the text if you knew that:

- **a** the writer wrote it in pain, in bed, with a lifelong illness?
- **b** the writer was a happily married family man?
- **c** the writer was a spy for the British government?
- **d** the novel was written in the year that World War I started?

## What you get marks for

| | |
|---|---|
| Half a mark each for details that suggest the historical period | 2 marks |
| 1 mark for each of 3 ways in which the maleness of the writer is suggested | 3 marks |
| 1 mark for seeing where and how the historical information may have a bearing on the text in each case | 4 marks |
| **Total** | **10 marks** |

# Answers

## Does context matter?

It is an extract from *The Trial*, a novel by Franz Kafka, translated from German. Franz Kafka was prone to deep depressions. He wrote his novels between the wars, when fascism was on the rise. This book was the last one he wrote before dying of tuberculosis in 1924.

Statements b, c, e, f and g are true.

## Authors

**A** From *Baggage*, the autobiography of Janet Street-Porter, a female Londoner

**B** From *An Evil Cradling* by Brian Keenan, an Irishman

**C** From *There is a Happy Land* by Keith Waterhouse, a working-class man from the north of England

*The Publishers would like to thank the following for permission to reproduce copyright material:*

**Copyright text and extract sources: pp.1, 7** and **33** *Only a Matter of Time: A Story from Kosovo* © Stewart Ross 2001, Hodder Children's Books. Reproduced by permission of Hodder and Stoughton Limited; **pp.6** and **69** 'Padfoot', 'The Christmas Trees' and 'Beautiful' from *Nightcomers* © Susan Price 1997, Hodder Children's Books. Reproduced by permission of Hodder and Stoughton Limited; **p.9** *The Divorce Express* © Paula Danziger 1982, Hodder Children's Books. Reproduced by permission of Hodder and Stoughton Limited; **p.10** *Stuck in Neutral* © Terry Trueman 2000, Hodder Children's Books. Reproduced by permission of Hodder and Stoughton Limited; **p.11** *Strays Like Us* © Richard Peck 1999, Hodder Children's Books; **pp.12** and **32** *Scorched* © Josephine Poole 2003, Hodder Children's Books. Reproduced by permission of Hodder and Stoughton Limited; **pp.13, 15** and **18** *The Fortune Teller* © Alison Prince 2001, Hodder Children's Books. Reproduced by permission of Hodder and Stoughton Limited; **p.17** *The Raven Waits* © June Oldham 1979, Hodder Children's Books; **p.17** *Witch Hunt* © Chris Priestley 2003, Hodder Children's Books; **pp.21, 23–25** and **28–29** *The Ivy Crown* © Gill Vickery 2001, Hodder Children's Books. Reproduced by permission of Hodder and Stoughton Limited; **pp.26–27** and **30** *The Ice Boy* © Patricia Elliott 2002, Hodder Children's Books. Reproduced by permission of Hodder and Stoughton Limited; **p.31** *Tread Softly* © Kate Pennington 2003, Hodder Children's Books; **pp.32, 34** and **60** *Daisy Chain Dream* © Joan O'Neill 1994, Hodder Children's Books. Reproduced by permission of Hodder and Stoughton Limited; **p.36** 'The Devil's Thumb' from *Eiger Dreams: Ventures Among Men and Mountains* © Jon Krakauer 1990, Dell; **pp.41–42** *Out of India* © Jamila Gavin 1997, Hodder Children's Books. Reproduced by permission of Hodder and Stoughton Limited; **p.50** facts from *XY: Toolkit for Life* © Matt Whyman 2004, Hodder Children's Books; **pp.53–54** *The Rules of Work* © Richard Templar 2002, Pearson Education Limited; **pp.57–58, 79, 81** and **84** 'The Dreamer', 'Hiders Can Find' and 'The Landing Window' from *Hauntings* © Susan Price 1995, Hodder Children's Books. Reproduced by permission of Hodder and Stoughton Limited; **p.59** *Bread and Sugar* © Joan O'Neill 1990, Hodder Children's Books. Reproduced by permission of Hodder and Stoughton Limited; **p.62** from *The Da Vinci Code* by Dan Brown, published by Bantam Press. Reprinted by permission of The Random House Group Ltd; **pp.63, 65** and **71** from *Touching the Void* by Joe Simpson, published by Jonathan Cape. Reprinted by permission of The Random House Group Ltd; **p.64** from *Something Might Happen* by Julie Myerson, published by Vintage. Reprinted by permission of The Random House Group Ltd; **p.66** *Fleshmarket* © Nicola Morgan 2003, Hodder Children's Books. Reproduced by permission of Hodder and Stoughton Limited; **p.69** *World War I True Stories* © Clive Gifford 2002, Hodder Children's Books; **p.69** *The Ghost of Thomas Kempe* © Penelope Lively 1973, Mammoth; **p.69** *On the Heights* © Walter Bonatti 1964, Rupert Hart-Davis; **p.69** from unknown source by Robert Spence Watson 1870; **p.72** *Mirror, Mirror* © Ed Drummond 1973, Sierra Book Clubs; **p.78** 'The inner man' by Christine M. Banks (entry in Mini-sagas competition) © Telegraph Group Limited 1985, 1999; **p.87** *The Trial* by Franz Kafka 1925; **p.88** *Baggage: My Childhood* © Janet Street-Porter 2004, Headline. Reproduced by permission of Headline Book Publishing Limited; **p.89** from *An Evil Cradling* by Brian Keenan, published by Hutchinson. Reprinted by permission of The Random House Group Ltd; **p.89** *There is a Happy Land* © Keith Waterhouse 1968, Longman; **p.90** *The Thirty-Nine Steps* by John Buchan 1914.

**Copyright photos and image sources: p.9** cover image of *The Divorce Express* © Hodder Children's Books, 1982. Reproduced by permission of Hodder and Stoughton Limited; **p.10** cover image of *Stuck in Neutral* © Hodder Children's Books, 2001. Reproduced by permission of Hodder and Stoughton Limited; **p.14** Adrian Sherratt/Alamy; **p.16** Universal/DNA/Working Title/The Kobal Collection/Mountain, Peter; **p.17** © Paul Edmondson/Corbis; **p.26** Des Kilfeather/Alamy; **p.29** Trevor Smithers ARPS/Alamy; **p.35** advert for Nikon D70 digital SLR camera © Nikon; **p.35** advert for Seiko Arctura Kinetic Chronograph Titanium watch © Seiko UK; **p.36** © Pat O'Hara/Corbis; **p.39** advert for production of *Beyond Reasonable Doubt* at The Yvonne Arnaud Theatre, Guildford © Stage Further Productions Ltd; **p.41** Getty Images; **p.42** Getty Images; **p.44** Gary Cook/Alamy; **p.44** David Wall/Alamy; **pp.44** and **47–48** 'Oases' and 'Paper' pages from *Oxford Children's Encyclopedia* Volume 5, second edition revised (OUP, 2004), copyright © Oxford University Press 1991, reprinted by permission of Oxford University Press; **p.49** © Jean Miele/Corbis; **p.50** © Louie Psihoyos/Corbis; **p.51** Andrew Fox/Alamy; **p.53** © Darama/Corbis; **p.61** Moviestore Collection Ltd; **p.62** Douglas Armand/Alamy; **p.64** Time Life Pictures/Getty Images; **p.67** cover image of *Gazza: My Story* © Headline, 2005; **p.67** cover image of *Shockwave* © John Murray, 2005; **p.67** cover image of *Who runs this place?* © John Murray, 2005; **p.68** Directphoto.org/Alamy; **p.72** Leslie Garland Picture Library/Alamy; **p.73** Edmonds/Fox 2000/The Kobal Collection; **p.74** Two Arts/CD/The Kobal Collection; **p.77** Mary Evans Picture Library; **p.82** Robert Harding Picture Library Ltd/Alamy; **p.85** Time Life Pictures/Getty Images; **p.86** Everett Collection/Rex Features; **p.86** Renn/Burrill/SFP/The Kobal Collection; **p.86** Moviestore Collection Ltd; **p.91** Getty Images.

*Every effort has been made to trace all copyright holders, but if any have been inadvertently overlooked the Publishers will be pleased to make the necessary arrangements at the first opportunity.*

Although every effort has been made to ensure that website addresses are correct at time of going to press, Hodder Murray cannot be held responsible for the content of any website mentioned in this book. It is sometimes possible to find a relocated web page by typing in the address of the home page for a website in the URL window of your browser.